Editorial Project Manager
Heather Douglas

Editor in Chief
Karen J. Goldfluss, M.S. Ed.

Creative Director
Sarah M. Fournier

Cover Artist
Diem Pascarella

Illustrator
Clint McKnight

Art Coordinator
Renée Mc Elwee

Imaging
Amanda R. Harter

Publisher
Mary D. Smith, M.S. Ed.

Author
Robert Smith

CORRELATED TO
CCSS & NGSS

For correlations to the Common Core State Standards, see page 159 of this book or visit *http://www.teachercreated.com/standards/*. For correlations to the Next Generation Science Standards, see page 160.

Teacher Created Resources

12621 Western Avenue
Garden Grove, CA 92841
www.teachercreated.com
ISBN: 978-1-4206-3966-7
©2016 Teacher Created Resources
Made in U.S.A.

Teacher Created Resources

CONTENTS

Introduction

PROJECT-BASED LEARNING

As educators, we are being required to place more emphasis on science, technology, engineering, and math (STEM) to ensure that today's students will be prepared for their future careers. Additionally, it is important that children learn and practice the 21st-century skills of collaboration, critical thinking, problem solving, and digital literacy in their daily curricula. These collaborative skills are imperative for students to learn, but they are not without challenges. *Stepping into STEM* provides students with needed practice in these areas.

Project-based learning, simply put, is learning by doing. Project-based learning, or PBL, tends to be deeper learning that is more relevant to students, and thus it is remembered longer. We need to educate students to be global competitors; and to do so, we must help them to think creatively, take risks, and put what they are learning into practice. After all, it doesn't do much good to know a formula if you don't know when to use it. Students also need to learn the value of failure as a learning experience. Some of the ideas and efforts they will make during an activity will not work. This can turn into a very positive experience since knowing what won't work, and why, may lead to the discovery of what will work!

Reading informational material provides needed background, but *doing* makes the difference. Concepts, ideas, and experiences of hands-on activities remain lodged in the brain for retrieval when needed.

In STEM curriculum, project-based learning is a must! Its collaborative style guarantees that 21st-century skills are fully integrated into the curriculum while supporting students' academic and socio-emotional growth. Furthermore, PBL allows teachers to assess what students comprehend immediately and adapt curriculum accordingly. Most of the activities in this book require more than just one person in order to successfully achieve the objectives.

CONNECTING SCIENCE, TECHNOLOGY, ENGINEERING, AND MATH

STEM activities blend four essential and related learning experiences into one activity. The science project provides the platform for engineering design experiences in virtually every activity. For example, a science activity dealing with the motion of a pendulum involves learning elements of engineering design to achieve the best results. Technology—both simple and high-tech—provides the framework and recording information. Some of the technology is related to the materials and techniques used in constructing the pendulum; computers are effective in recording and comparing results. The math element will involve comparisons expressed in decimals, fractions, ratios, and percentages, as well as measurements, graphs, charts, and other visual representations.

THE NEED FOR INTERACTION AND COLLABORATION

Today's scientists share ideas, experiences, and experiments with colleagues as close as their own university, as well as at great distances across the globe.

Student scientists, like professional scientists, need experience working with partners in a collaborative and supportive environment. They need to exchange ideas, test theories, perform experiments, modify their experiments, try novel approaches—even those that may not appear useful or serious—and cooperate with each other in all aspects of the project as they seek to accomplish their objectives. This process is often referred to as "The Design Process." The Design Process mini poster on the next page can be posted or copied for each student.

A basic requirement of this collaborative effort is a willingness to seriously consider all suggestions from the members of the team. Ideas should be considered, tried, tested, and compared for use in the project. Students should work together to select the most efficient and practical ideas and then methodically test each one for its useful application in the activity.

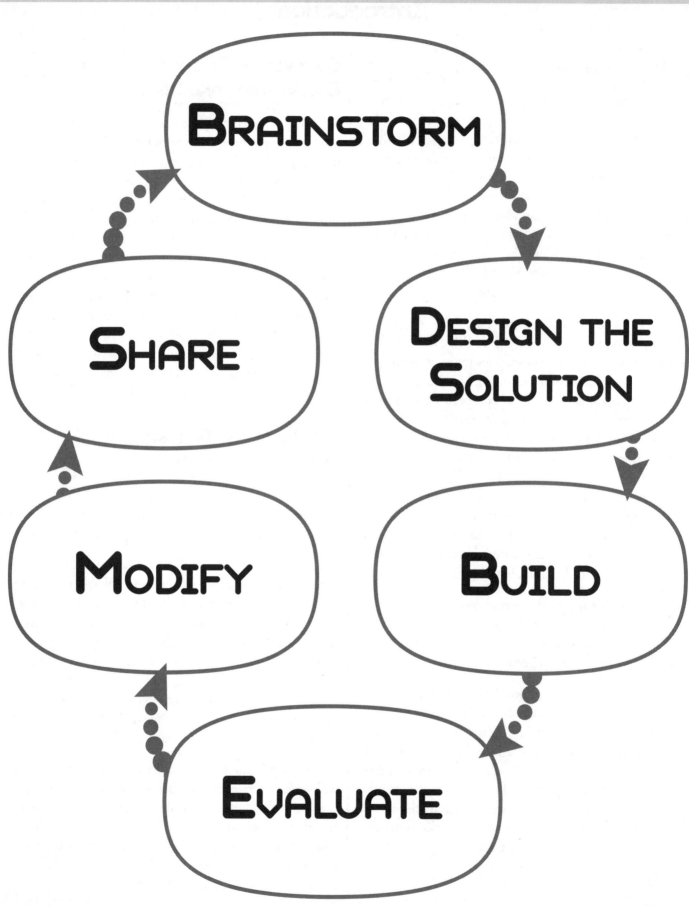

THE DESIGN PROCESS WORKSHEET

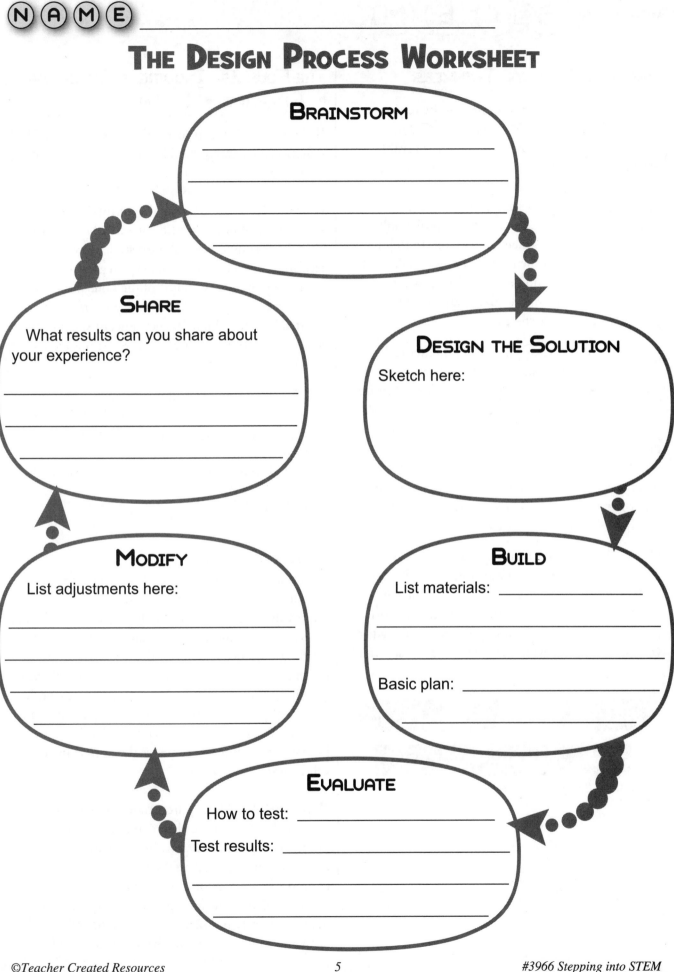

BRAINSTORM

_____
_____
_____
_____

SHARE

What results can you share about your experience?

_____
_____
_____

DESIGN THE SOLUTION

Sketch here:

MODIFY

List adjustments here:

_____
_____
_____

BUILD

List materials: _____
_____
_____

Basic plan: _____
_____

EVALUATE

How to test: _____

Test results: _____
_____
_____

GROWING CRITICAL THINKERS

While all members of a team need to be respected and heard, members of the team also need to critically examine each idea to see if it is feasible. Students need to apply their learned experiences in these activities, and their serious attention should be given to testing each idea for feasibility and practicality. Students can develop this skill by considering each serious suggestion, testing it for workability, and then determining its value. Students need to examine the available materials, work with them in an organized way, record their results, and compare these results.

Critical thinkers are organized and methodical in their testing. They examine the ideas generated in the free flow of comments and discussions. Critical thinkers determine which ideas can be tested and then carefully compared for useful application to the problem they are trying to solve. They keep an open mind. Critical thinkers base their judgments on observations and proven outcomes. Critical thinkers aren't negative, but they are skeptical until they observe the results of an activity.

One of the hallmarks of a scientist is to ask questions. Another is the effort to seek answers through effective investigations, tests, and experiments. You want to encourage your student scientists to practice critical thinking by asking thoughtful questions using academic vocabulary, and developing creative ways to test possible solutions.

"Show me."   "Let's check it out."

"How can we test it to see if it works?"

THE FOUR IS: INQUIRE • INVESTIGATE • INTERACT • INVENT

The four basic elements of an effective science or STEM activity can be categorized as Inquiry, Investigation, Interaction, and Invention.

1. INQUIRY is the process of determining what you wish to learn about a scientific or natural phenomenon. It can be as simple as watching a student's swing move back and forth, observing a schoolyard game of marbles, or sucking on a straw. Some of the same principles of science may apply to a helicopter rescue of a swimmer, a batted ball in a major-league game, or the process of getting water out of a ditch. The questions are always the same:

"Why did it happen? Will it happen every time? What happens if . . . you change the length of the swing, the size of the marble, the diameter of the straw, the weight of the swimmer, the diameter of the ball, or the size of the siphon hose in the ditch?"

In the simplest form, **Inquire** is a question: Why . . . ?, What if . . . ?, How . . . ?

2. INVESTIGATION is the action a scientist takes to learn more about the question. It involves the process a student scientist needs to follow. The investigation can involve background research, the process of doing an experiment, and the interpretation of the results. Reading a science text about the workings of the pendulum is not the same as actually constructing a working pendulum, adjusting it to different lengths and weights, and carefully observing its features and behavior in varying circumstances. Measuring these in mathematical terms provides the opportunity for valid comparisons as well.

3. INTERACTION requires student scientists to work with one or more classmates to assess the problem or question, determine the nature of the investigation, and analyze the results, looking for the most reasonable or useful course of action. Most detailed scientific experiments require more than two hands and benefit from the shared input of two or more actively involved minds.

The Four *Is* (cont.)

From a practical point of view, experiments done with students are more effective with teams of two. In larger groups, one or more team members often feel left out, don't get to actually do the hands-on construction, and often end up in distracting behaviors. Teams of two require the active involvement of both individuals in all phases of the activity all the time. An off-task student in a team can be refocused by a partner or the teacher.

It is important to have enough materials and equipment for the basic activity for each team. The materials used in the activities in this book are inexpensive and easily available to facilitate two-person teams.

4. Invention is the final stage of the 4 "*Is*" in which the science activity involves the effort to create or invent a solution, modification, or improvement. This can be the most challenging aspect of the activity. Suggestions, at first, tend to be far out, impractical, silly, or impossible to do with the available materials. The most effective teams discuss possible solutions and then start manipulating the materials as a form of "thinking with their hands."

The invention aspect of the activity is nearly always the final step of the activity. For instance, after multiple sessions manipulating and measuring results with a pendulum, students should have enough background and hands-on experience to invent an application for this tool. It may be a toy swing for a doll, a time-keeping mechanism for a class activity such as a timed math exercise, or an attempt to make a perpetual-motion machine (or one that just lasts longer than anybody else's).

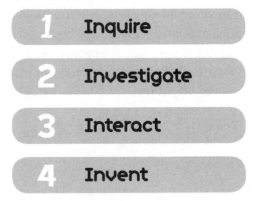

The Need for Journaling

Scientists keep records. They are meticulous in recording the results of their investigations and often refer back to investigations done in previous months and years. They use this information as needed for further investigations, related experiments, and in publishing their work.

Ideally, all science students should keep a journal recording the investigations they have been working on. With continued practice, students will develop the habit of journaling after each period of investigation. It is helpful to use 3-ring binders for the students' pages from this book, including the journal entries. It is easier for students to keep information in one place and to refer back to previous investigations for discussion purposes and records. Daily spiral notebooks, composition books, or 3-ring binders can also be used.

It is suggested that a separate entry be made for each investigation session. Have students enter the date and investigation title or stage on each new entry. Include the key question for each activity. This is the starting point for each investigation. As students proceed through each unit, they should record— using adequate details—the process and materials used to investigate the question. Encourage students to use appropriate vocabulary when journaling.

The variations in technique, the engineering adjustments, the technology employed, and the results of each modification should be recorded. The mathematical applications should also be noted. If the length of the pendulum fishing line was doubled or cut in half, this is critical information. If the weight was doubled from 8 grams to 16 grams, this should be noted, and the effect on the pendulum's swing distance and duration should be recorded. The results of each trial should be briefly recorded.

The most important information in the journal should be the conclusions of the research team about the answer to the testable questions the team was investigating. Individual researchers may draw separate conclusions about these questions, but the conclusions need to be based on objective facts and recorded information.

THE DESIGN PROCESS REVIEW

The journal entries should be the "notes" student scientists use when sharing their information during the class discussion called "The Design Process Review." The teacher should act as the moderator of this discussion and ensure that all students get an opportunity to share their experiences, results, and scientific observations. These discussions work well as a 10-minute closure activity at the end of each period.

Encourage all students to take turns sharing the results of their activities and the conclusions they drew from their experiments. Data summaries may include photos, videos, or other relevant materials.

Model and encourage serious reporting. Encourage students to incorporate new vocabulary into their discussions, their journaling, and their presentation pieces.

The writing (journaling) and the review are vital elements in the design process. They provide students with the opportunity to share their experiences, and they serve as an excellent part of the assessment process. It is suggested that you allow at least 15 to 20 minutes to complete these activities.

You may choose to act as a moderator. You can allow students to share as teams or individuals about each activity and others they have done on related subjects. You may also use smaller groups with student moderators.

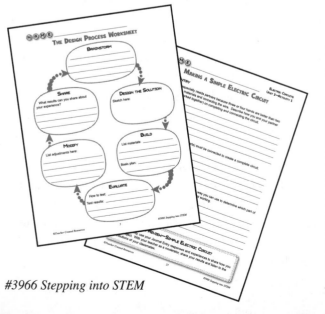

KEEPING THINGS IN PERSPECTIVE!

A STEM class will rarely be perfectly quiet! In fact, the low buzz of purposeful conversation is an indicator that students are actively engaged. The teacher serves as the facilitator, providing guidance, crucial information, and directions at the outset. It is important to regularly check on each group to offer encouragement, advice, correction, and support.

Teachers need to evaluate how students are doing as teams proceed with investigations. In addition to guiding the learning process, it is also very important to draw closure on the activity by moderating the final portion of the Design Process Review where you draw conclusions and highlight the core learning concepts embedded in the activity.

Unsuccessful periods happen in any class, no matter how capable the instructor or how gifted the students. Things can go wrong, bells ring forever, announcements from the intercom break the flow of instruction and construction, and all the other distractions of school life can occur. You may get a true scientific discussion going, only to have it go off into areas unrelated to the thrust of the investigation.

But there are also those times when you encounter the pleasant experience of no one paying any attention to the distraction. A visitor or principal enters the room, observes the activity for a moment, and either leaves or joins a group. The science discussion reverts to the main idea and goes smoothly or vigorously along, driven by students who are focused and on task. Yes, it happens!

Students can really "get into" science. They enjoy the openness involved in the activity, the collegial nature of working on a project, the materials they get to manipulate, and the mental stimulation of solving a problem or creating a better product. A good, productive, stimulating science period can make their day—and yours, too.

How to Use This Book

Stepping into STEM is arranged with flexibility in mind. One method is to move from lesson to lesson in each unit and proceed through the units in order. However, the number and order of units completed throughout the year is completely dependent on classroom and curriculum needs. You may want to choose the activities with which you are more familiar or those that fit your school schedule better. The organization of each unit moves from a teacher-directed initial activity, through two or three more open-ended activities, to a final challenge activity that allows students to create their own unique "invention." The final unit in the book is longer and more complicated in scope and involves a culminating activity that challenges student minds and helps draw closure.

Pacing Units and Lessons

Planning the length of time for completion of each unit can be flexible. You may choose some or all of the units and pace them througout the year, building each unit into your science curriculum. If a unit topic fits in well with what is currently being taught, embed it into the schedule where possible. Since these unit investigations were developed to foster a STEM approach to learning, they do not have to be tied to any specific time frame or topic in the science curriculum.

To get the most out of a unit, it is suggested that a few sessions be allotted to complete the activities. These can be spread out as needed. Usually, an activity can be done in about an hour. For those fortunate enough to have a one-and-a-half-hour period, students will have more time to explore the variations in each project and extend their creative explorations. Remember that the unit activities can be broken into more than one session! Be sure to allow serious time for both journaling and recording information within each period.

Vocabulary and Discussions

Share and discuss unit vocabulary lists with students. Identify and use the terms frequently throughout the sessions to reinforce essential subject-area vocabulary.

Enlarge each list to create posters for student reference, or photocopy the list for each student to keep in his or her journaling notebooks.

Encourage discussions within groups and between groups if they are focused on the topic. Also allow some time for the teacher-moderated colloquium in which individuals share their experiments, results, and conclusions based on their research.

A general activity period could allow 5 to 7 minutes for teacher introduction and review of previous learning, 5 minutes to efficiently distribute supplies, and 30 to 40 minutes to complete the activity involving science, technology, engineering, and math. The remaining time should be devoted to science journaling.

Teacher and Student Rubrics

Use the teacher rubric on page 16 to evaluate team progress, time-on-task, student interaction, and to reinforce STEM objectives. Students who are focused on the objective and methodically trying different ways to solve a problem are doing science. So are those who are responding a bit randomly to their own ideas and trying them out.

As student groups work through each investigation, they should complete the student rubric on page 17 to reinforce the processes they used and to reflect on the procedures they followed.

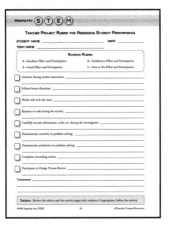

NOTE: Explain both rubrics to students before starting the units. It is important for them to know how their work will be evaluated and what steps they should follow as they work on a unit investigation.

CHALLENGE ACTIVITY

Each of the seven major units has a challenge activity as the last activity. Students are given lists of suggested materials and advised to look over their journals about previous activities in the unit for hints and ideas. For example, students doing the bridge activity are challenged to build a suspension bridge. Students will have noticed in previous experiments which aspects of the different bridges held the biggest loads and which materials held up the best.

There are also some directions/suggestions in each Challenge lesson to guide students who need them. Allow time for frustration, imagination, and so forth to set in during the building period for each of these challenge assignments. Use the grading rubric for creativity, success, effort, and on-task work time.

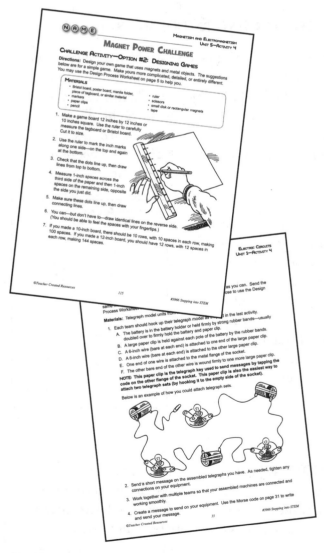

TEAM MANAGEMENT AND MATERIALS

In this explosive era of scientific knowledge and discovery, teamwork matters; all children need the kinesthetic experiences and collaborative interaction with their peers that are essential aspects of science instruction.

The activities in this series were designed to maximize student participation. Students will work in pairs or small collaborative teams. The collaborative process is essential to construct the apparatus and create the models. *Four hands and two minds working together are more efficient and effective than individuals proceeding alone.*

Materials used for the STEM activities in this book are not from expensive science kits. Those kits tend to not provide enough materials to engage all students simultaneously. Virtually all of the materials used in this series are available at relatively inexpensive cost at local big-box and discount stores. Other materials are available in local hardware or craft stores.

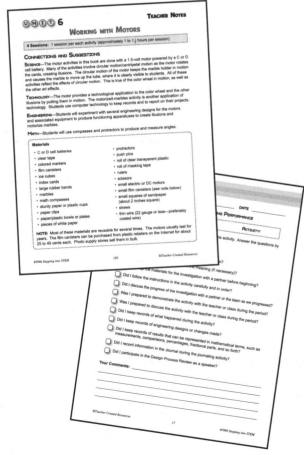

Lesson Notes for the Teacher

LESSON 1 — GUIDED ACTIVITY

The first lesson is designed so that the teacher can guide and control the pace of the activity and ensure that students know how to function in this type of science activity and with these materials. It is more teacher-directed in terms of time and following specific directions than later lessons in the unit.

Providing guidance through the beginning phases of each unit will set the stage for student groups to continue with their investigations and discussions throughout the units. This is also an opportunity for the teacher to note which teams or students might be struggling, and to provide more assistance to them.

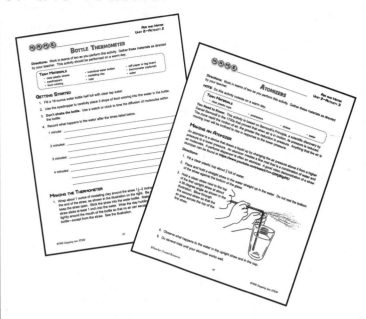

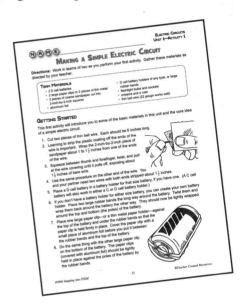

FINAL LESSON — THE CHALLENGE

The final lesson in each unit involves a Challenge Activity in which students apply what they learned in earlier lessons to solving a specific problem or making the fastest, best, or most unique applications of the concepts learned. Students work in pairs.

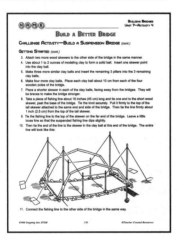

LESSONS — YOUR TURN

Review students' findings and ideas related to their investigations in Activity 1. Discuss how students will be exploring how a project works under various conditions. This can be an independent collaborative group activity. Students work in pairs.

The second and third lessons (and sometimes a fourth) allow students to work at their own pace as they do the lesson. The teacher circulates through the room giving advice, encouragement, and correction as needed. Students work in pairs.

ABOUT TEAMS

Although there are always students who prefer to work alone—and have difficulty working with others—most students quickly find that these projects need 3 or 4 hands working in unison to work well. Most students also realize that the opportunity to share ideas and experiences helps their own performance and is reflected in their success in a project.

You may want to have students switch partners when you start a new unit or after partners have been together for a few units.

ABOUT TEAMS *(cont.)*

Whenever possible, keep the teams small (two people) and therefore able to keep their hands and minds occupied and on task.

The activities in this series are designed for full participation by all students with all students actively engaged at all times. All students will use the materials and should have access to the necessary equipment. Students work in collaborative teams in order to facilitate learning, but all students are actively engaged with all aspects of the projects.

The collaborative process is essential in constructing the apparatus and creating models because four hands and two minds working together are more efficient and effective than individuals proceeding alone. In this age of the explosion of scientific knowledge and discovery, there are very few lone scientists working in private anymore. Teamwork matters—and all children need the kinesthetic experiences and collaborative interaction with their peers that are essential aspects of science instruction.

ELL TIPS

Review vocabulary with ELLs (English Language Learners) to assure understanding. Ask ELLs to describe the intent and focus of the project. Pair ELLs with EO (English Only) students where needed. Strongly encourage the journaling and discussion aspect of the activities.

A Note About Materials

The materials used in these projects are quite inexpensive, easy to locate or order, and in most cases, reusable. Some are simply school supplies. There should be a sufficient supply for each team. Virtually all of the materials used in this series are available at relatively inexpensive cost in local stores—especially wholesale places and some dollar discount stores. A few are available in local hardware stores.

See individual units for a listing of specific materials. Be sure to collect all materials ahead of time; consider ways to distribute, use, and store materials prior to introducing each new unit. If possible, establish an area in the classroom where materials can be accessed easily.

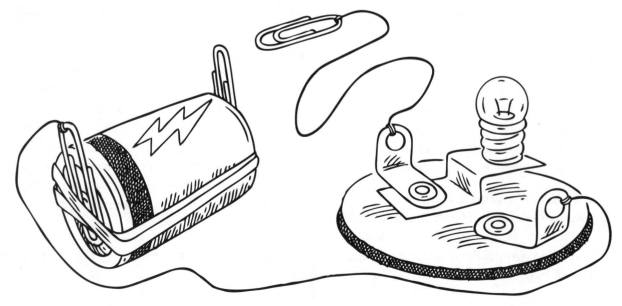

Addressing Standards

NEXT GENERATION SCIENCE STANDARDS

The National Research Council of the National Academy of Sciences published "A Framework for K–12 Science Education: Practices, Crosscutting Concepts, and Core Ideas."

Its purpose was to serve as a guide for the states presently collaborating to develop the Next Generation Science Standards. The framework defined *science* to mean "the traditional natural sciences: physics, chemistry, biology, and (more recently) earth, space, and environmental sciences."

The council used the term *engineering* to mean "any engagement in a systematic practice of design to achieve solutions to particular human problems."

They used the term *technology* "to include all types of human-made systems and processes—not just in the limited sense often used in schools that equates technology with modern computational and communications devices. Technologies result when engineers apply their understanding of the natural world and of human behavior to design ways to satisfy human needs and wants." (NRC 2012, p. 11–12)

One of the critical elements of the Next Generation Science Standards is the effort to develop science practices in students. These are the behaviors that scientists actually engage in as they do their investigations. When students or scientists engage in science, they are deeply involved in inquiry as they use a range of skills and knowledge at the same time.

The engineering practices "are the behaviors that engineers engage in as they apply science and math to design solutions to problems." Engineering design has similarities to scientific inquiry. However, there are differences in the two subjects:

- Scientific inquiry involves creating a question that can be solved through investigation, such as, "What might happen if I only used hot water to make a cloud?"

- Engineering design involves creating a question that can be solved through design.

    "How can I make a faster motor?"

    "What happens to my invention when I add another motor?"

These are engineering questions although they may produce scientific information. Strengthening the engineering component in these standards helps students recognize the interrelationship between the four cornerstones of STEM instruction: Science, Technology, Engineering, and Math.

The **Disciplinary Core Ideas (DCI)** in the Next Generation Science Standards are broad essential ideas in science instruction across several grade levels and areas of science instruction (including the life sciences, earth and space science, the physical sciences, engineering, and technology).

Cross-cutting Concepts are ideas that bridge the boundaries between science and engineering and that help students connect different ideas in the sciences into a recognizable pattern. They provide students with an organizational framework for connecting science and engineering concepts into coherent patterns.

The 7 Cross-cutting Concepts

1. Patterns
2. Cause and Effect
3. Scale, Proportion, and Quantity
4. Systems and System Models
5. Energy and Matter
6. Structure and Function
7. Stability and Change

Most good science activities exhibit examples of several of these concepts, of course, and students should begin to notice these concepts as they do the experiments in this book. Their journals should specify one or more of these concepts as they write about a project.

Addressing Standards

COMMON CORE STATE STANDARDS

The math applications needed to do complete, detailed science activities are as essential as the apparatus and materials used in the activities. The emphasis on math and reading literacy is built into the Common Core as a prominent aspect of the near-national consensus that Common Core provides. The application of both skills is essential to STEM teaching.

Teachers may find that they need to explain the application of a wide variety of math concepts as these concepts arise in STEM activities. These math activities may involve measurement, computing percentages, working with fractions and mixed numbers, measuring and converting units of time, measuring and comparing distances, working with metric units, and many other math concepts. Students often know the processes in these math activities but have no idea how to use them in real-life or scientific applications.

The Common Core State Standards have placed a strong emphasis on math *applications*, not just the mechanics of a skill. Utilizing math in comparing various results in a science activity will increase understanding of many concepts. Metric measurement, the common system used in science, becomes second nature to students who routinely use it to measure and compare distance, volume, and capacity, for example. Percentages, ratios, and other comparative measurements have more meaning when applied to hands-on activities.

The Common Core Standards are likewise focused on informational reading in science (as well as social studies). Students need to become familiar with sources beyond the textbook to research science information. These involve both paper and digital sources.

The writing standards of the Common Core also expect students to routinely write effectively on science topics. The activities in this book provide a guided opportunity to take notes and write brief reports on each activity while including all relevant details.

Common Core State Standards emphasize the development of speaking and listening skills, and they encourage discussion and collaboration. *Stepping into STEM* provides opportunities for students to use their collective writings with each other in discussions.

STANDARDS CORRELATIONS

Correlations for both the Common Core State Standards and the Next Generation Science Standards are provided for the units in this book.

General standards correlations for each can be found on pages 159–160. You can also visit *www.teachercreated.com/standards* for more comprehensive correlations charts for the Common Core State Standards.

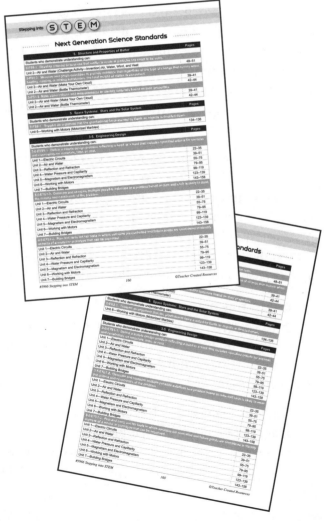

STEM VOCABULARY

apparatus—an instrument or set of materials designed for a specific use

analyze—to examine critically and in careful detail

assess—to estimate or make a judgment about

brainstorm—a technique used to solve problems in which members of a group share their ideas about a subject

collaborate—to work with one or more members in a team

component—an important piece or ingredient

confer—to have discussions and exchange opinions

design—to form or conceive in the mind; plan

efficient—working well without an unusual amount of effort

evaluate—to make a judgment

hypothesis—a serious scientific guess or idea

investigate—to observe or study by close examination and systematic inquiry

manipulate—to handle easily with the hands

modify—to change or adjust some qualities while keeping other qualities the same

observations—scientific information observed during an experiment

source—a point of origin

strategize—to make a plan to achieve a goal

systematic—done according to a fixed plan

troubleshoot—to find a solution to a problem or disagreement

TEACHER RUBRIC FOR ASSESSING STUDENT PERFORMANCE

STUDENT NAME _____ DATE _____

TEAM NAME _____

SCORING RUBRIC

4—Excellent Effort and Participation   **2**—Satisfactory Effort and Participation

3—Good Effort and Participation   **1**—Poor or No Effort and Participation

☐ Attentive during teacher instruction _____
_____

☐ Follows lesson directions _____
_____

☐ Works well with the team _____
_____

☐ Remains on task during the activity _____
_____

☐ Carefully records information, trials, etc. during the investigation _____
_____

☐ Demonstrates creativity in problem solving _____
_____

☐ Demonstrates persistence in problem solving _____
_____

☐ Completes journaling entries _____
_____

☐ Participates in Design Process Review _____
_____

Comments: _____
_____
_____

Teachers: Review the rubrics and the activity pages with students, if appropriate, before the activity.

NAME _____ DATE _____

Student Rubric for Assessing Performance

Unit:	Activity:

Directions: Use this rubric to guide you as you work on the activity. Answer the questions by placing an "X" in each box as you go along.

☐ Did I read the project instructions carefully?

☐ Did I discuss the instructions with a partner or the team?

☐ Did I confer with another team about the meaning (if necessary)?

☐ Did I set up the materials for the investigation with a partner before beginning?

☐ Did I follow the instructions in the activity carefully and in order?

☐ Did I discuss the progress of the investigation with a partner or the team as we progressed?

☐ Was I prepared to demonstrate the activity with the teacher or class during the period?

☐ Was I prepared to discuss the activity with the teacher or class during the period?

☐ Did I keep records of what happened during the activity?

☐ Did I keep records of engineering designs or changes made?

☐ Did I keep records of results that can be represented in mathematical terms, such as measurements, comparisons, percentages, fractional parts, and so forth?

☐ Did I record information in the Journal during the journaling activity?

☐ Did I participate in the Design Process Review as a speaker?

Your Comments: _____

_____

_____

_____

_____

ELECTRIC CIRCUITS

4 Sessions: 1 session per each activity (approximately 1 to $1\frac{1}{2}$ hours per session)

CONNECTIONS AND SUGGESTIONS

SCIENCE—Students will explore different sources of electricity and the flow of electrons in a closed path of a complete circuit. They will build their own complete circuit using batteries as a voltage source, as well as explore real-world applications of circuits when they build a telegraph. They will also learn about the importance of conductors and nonconductors.

TECHNOLOGY—Students can use the Internet to research electricity and its different sources, as well as the circuits that are in many everyday devices. They may also research the discovery of electricity and its impact on technology throughout history, as well as the resulting communication technology. They may research images and diagrams of closed circuits and telegraphs in order to help them create the projects in each activity. Additionally, students can photograph or record their observations and responses as they create closed circuits and build telegraphs. They might also describe the problems encountered, the solutions attempted, the success rate of each activity, different approaches used, and suggestions for improvement. This can be done in an online journal, blog, or even in a simple Word document.

ENGINEERING—Students will use the design process to create a variety of electrical circuit designs. They will be able to test the most effective combination of supplies and troubleshoot when a circuit is incomplete and/or the light bulb doesn't light. A discussion can ensue regarding how electrical engineers design the circuits and batteries in the devices and appliances we use every day.

MATH—This unit requires students to measure lengths of wire as part of the setup instructions for most of the electrical experiments. They will also record their observations using charts and diagrams. Students can also determine the ratio of bulbs lit to batteries used.

Materials

- 1 box of 100 large paper clips
- 5 sheets of coarse sandpaper (for stripping the rubber-coated ends of the bell wire)
- D cell batteries
- flashlight bulbs
- flashlight bulb sockets
- 100 feet of thin insulated electrical "bell wire" (22 gauge works well)

- AA and AAA batteries
- C cell batteries
- D cell battery holders or large rubber bands
- aluminum foil
- rulers
- scissors

Optional:

- large steel or iron nails
- wire stripper or pliers

NOTE: Most or all of this material is reusable several times.

• UNIT I VOCABULARY •

apparatus—various components used to create an electrical circuit

circuit—an arrangement in which a flow of electricity travels from a source, such as a battery, to a use, such as lighting a bulb or sending a message

conductors—materials that transfer electrical energy from the source to the use, such as copper wire, steel, or aluminum

current—a flow of electricity along a circuit

electromagnet—a device that creates a magnetic field using the flow of electricity through a metal wire wrapped around an iron bar

electrons—negatively charged particles in an atom

insulators—materials that do not conduct electrical current; non-conductors of electricity such as cloth, rubber, or plastic

socket—a device for holding a bulb

source—a device, such as a battery, that produces electricity

flange—a rim or projecting edge that sticks out and is used for strength or for attachment to another object

DISCUSSION PROMPT:

Nowadays, we take electricity for granted. It's available at the touch of a button or the flip of a switch. But only a little over 100 years ago, most people still relied on kerosene lamps for light, ice boxes to keep food cool, and wood- or coal-burning stoves for heat. What are some electric devices that you rely on daily? How would your life be different without electricity to power these devices?

IT'S ELECTRIFYING!

Electricity is one of our most widely used forms of energy. We can witness it in nature when we see lightning flash or feel the shock of static electricity built up from friction. We even use electricity in our bodies by sending electrical signals from our brains to our muscles, telling them to move. We harness electricity—which is actually a secondary energy source—from the conversion of other sources of energy, such as coal, oil, natural gas, nuclear power, or the energy of running water (hydropower).

An electric circuit is a continuous, uninterrupted flow of an electric charge (electrons) from a source (such as a battery). This flow continues along a closed path (such as a wire) to an application (such as a light bulb) back to the source (battery). This flow of electric charge is called a current. When any part of the circuit is disconnected, the electric current stops. Have you ever had to change a light bulb? When a light bulb is broken or burnt out, it doesn't light because the circuit is open. When the old bulb is replaced with a new one, the circuit is closed and the electric charge can move through the circuit and light the bulb.

Electrical conductors are materials, such as copper or aluminum wire, through which an electric charge can flow. Electrical insulators (or nonconductors) break the flow of the electric charge, and an electric current does not flow. These include wood, plastic, rubber, and cloth. Many times you will see conductors and nonconductors used together for different applications. For example, electrical cords have wires that deliver the electricity from an outlet to a device, such as a television. However, they are covered with an insulator such as plastic or rubber so that the electricity can only move along the path of the wire. This keeps you safe if you need to touch the cord to move it or unplug it.

In this unit, you will be constructing closed circuits in order to light a light bulb. Most people associate the light bulb with the inventor Thomas Alva Edison. There were as many as 22 other inventors prior to Edison who also created some type of light bulb, but Edison was the first to make one that was long-lasting and practical for everyday use.

Another inventor that harnessed electricity in an invention was Samuel F.B. Morse. Morse developed and patented a telegraph that used electrical signals to transmit and receive messages over long distances. His assistant, Alfred Vail, helped him develop an alphabet of signals involving tones, lights, and clicks. These signals are a combination of short and long "dots" and "dashes" whose order determine the sequence of letters in a message. This method of signaling is called Morse code. You will be using Morse code to create sentences for others to translate using closed circuits.

ELECTRIC CIRCUITS

The information below will help you as you complete the activities in this unit.

Use a computer or tablet to search for information on the Internet to help you as you complete the activities in this unit. Helpful search terms include:

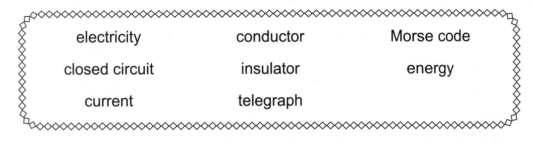

electricity	conductor	Morse code
closed circuit	insulator	energy
current	telegraph	

Below is an example of a simple closed circuit for lighting a light bulb. There are many arrangements that can be created with the supplies available to you.

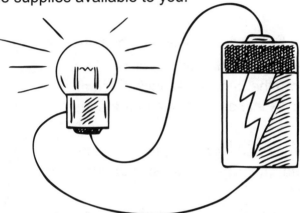

You will used the Morse Code below to create messages.

THE INTERNATIONAL MORSE CODE

A • –	J • – – –	S • • •
B – • • •	K – • –	T –
C – • – •	L • – • •	U • • –
D – • •	M – –	V • • • –
E •	N – •	W • – –
F • • – •	O – – –	X – • • –
G – – •	P • – – •	Y – • – –
H • • • •	Q – – • –	Z – – • •
I • •	R • – •	0 – – – – –
1 • – – – –	2 • • – – –	3 • • • – –
4 • • • • –	5 • • • • •	6 – • • • •
7 – – • • •	8 – – – • •	9 – – – – •

MAKING A SIMPLE ELECTRIC CIRCUIT

Directions: Work in teams of two as you perform your first activity. Gather these materials as directed by your teacher.

TEAM MATERIALS

- 2 D cell batteries
- 2 large paper clips or 2 pieces of thin metal
- 2 pieces of coarse sandpaper cut into 2-inch-by-2-inch squares
- aluminum foil
- D cell battery holders of any type, or large rubber bands
- flashlight bulbs and sockets
- scissors and a ruler
- thin bell wire (22 gauge works well)

GETTING STARTED

This first activity will introduce you to some of the basic materials in this unit and the core idea of a simple electric circuit.

1. Cut two pieces of thin bell wire. Each should be 6 inches long.

2. Learning to strip the plastic coating off the ends of the wire is important. Wrap the 2-inch-by-2-inch piece of sandpaper about 1 to $1\frac{1}{2}$ inches from one of the ends of the wire.

3. Squeeze between thumb and forefinger, twist, and pull at the wire covering until it pulls off, exposing about $1\frac{1}{2}$ inches of bare wire.

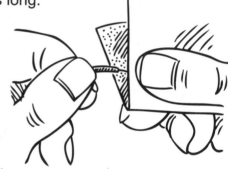

4. Use the same procedure on the other end of the wire. You and your partner need two wires with both ends stripped about $1\frac{1}{2}$ inches.

5. Place a D cell battery in a battery holder for that size battery, if you have one. (A C cell battery will also work in either a C or D cell battery holder.)

6. If you don't have a battery holder for either size battery, you can create your own battery holder. Place two large rubber bands the long way around the battery. Twist them and wrap them back around the battery the other way. They should now be tightly wrapped around the top and bottom (the poles) of the battery.

7. Place one large paper clip—or a thin metal paper holder—against the top of the battery and under the rubber bands so that the paper clip is held firmly in place. Cover the paper clip with a small piece of aluminum foil before you put it between the rubber bands and the top of the battery.

8. Do the same thing with the other large paper clip on the bottom of the battery. The paper clips (covered with aluminum foil) should be tightly held in place against the poles of the battery by the rubber bands.

N A M E _____

MAKING A SIMPLE ELECTRIC CIRCUIT

COMPLETING THE CIRCUIT

1. Carefully screw the small flashlight bulb into the bulb holder until it is firmly in place. (It will usually only require 2 or 3 turns.)

2. Wrap the bare end of one wire around the paper clip so that it is held firmly against the battery on one pole. Wrap the other end of the wire around one metal flange, tab, or screw that is on the bulb holder.

3. Wrap one end of the second wire around the paper clip on the other pole of the battery. Touch the other end of the second wire to the metal flange, tab, or screw that is on the bulb holder.

4. The bulb should light. Make sure all the wires are firmly attached and that the bulb lights and stays lit when the wires are in contact.

 _____

MAKING A SIMPLE ELECTRIC CIRCUIT

TRY THIS

1. There are several different arrangements that will provide a complete circuit and light the bulb. Try these arrangements and see which ones create a complete circuit and lights the bulb.

   a. both battery poles connected—1 socket flange unattached

   b. both socket flanges attached to 1 wire—both battery poles not connected

   c. 1 battery pole attached to 1 socket—the other battery pole unattached

   d. 1 battery pole attached to both sockets

2. Try to find out how many different connections can be made with the bulb still lighting.

   Each of the following parts must be in contact with the bare ends of the wire to form an electric circuit:

   a. top and bottom of the battery

   b. bottom and side of the bulb (in the metal parts of the socket)

   c. the battery and socket flanges

   Record your results below. The elevated head of the battery is called the *positive pole*. The flat bottom of the battery is called the *negative pole*.

   Draw simple sketches of the battery, socket, wire, and bulb in four different configurations and record the results for each.

   Label **Y** if it is a complete circuit and **N** if it is not a complete circuit.

1.   2.

   Complete? _____   Complete? _____

3.   4.

   Complete? _____   Complete? _____

 N A M E _____

MAKING A SIMPLE ELECTRIC CIRCUIT

JOURNAL ENTRY

1. This project especially needs partners because three or four hands are better than two for holding the materials and connecting the wire. Describe how you and your partner collaborated (worked together) on completing and connecting the circuit.

   _____

   _____

   _____

   _____

   _____

2. Describe what components (parts) must be connected to create a complete circuit.

   _____

   _____

   _____

   _____

   _____

3. If the bulb doesn't light, describe a systematic way you can use to determine which part of the circuit is burned out, broken, worn out, or not working.

   _____

   _____

   _____

   _____

   _____

DESIGN PROCESS REVIEW—SIMPLE ELECTRIC CIRCUIT

In this first activity, use your Journal Entry responses and experiences to share how you did the project. With your teacher as a moderator, share your results and listen to the contributions of your classmates.

CONDUCTORS AND INSULATORS

Directions: Work in teams of two as you perform this activity. Gather these materials as directed by your teacher.

TEAM MATERIALS

- 2 large paper clips or 2 pieces of thin metal
- AAA batteries
- AA batteries
- aluminum foil
- C cell batteries

- D cell batteries
- D cell battery holders of any type or large rubber bands
- flashlight bulbs and sockets
- thin bell wire (22 gauge works well)

NOTE TO TEACHER: The collection of batteries should include some that are new and others that are used or dead.

BATTERY CHECKER

1. Assemble your complete circuit apparatus as in Activity 1 or use your saved circuit from Activity 1.

   A. The battery is in a battery holder or tightly held by rubber bands.

   B. There are large metal pieces or large paper clips tightly held against the battery by the holder or rubber bands.

   C. There is a bulb holder or socket that has a bulb securely held by the socket.

   D. Both wires have bare ends about $1\frac{1}{2}$ inches on both ends of the wire.

   E. One wire is attached to one paper clip or metal piece at one end of the battery holder and to one of two metal pieces on the socket holder.

   F. The second wire is attached to the other metal piece on the socket holder.

   Touch the loose end of the second wire to the other paper clip on the battery.

   <u>The bulb should light.</u>

2. Test several batteries from the collection you and your teacher brought in. Try D cells, C cells, AAA batteries, and AA batteries in place of your battery. Be sure that the rubber band or your fingers hold the bare wire ends firmly against both ends of the battery.

3. Make three stacks of batteries—one for good batteries, one for dead batteries, and one for low-power batteries (that light the bulb dimly).

4. Trade your tested batteries and results with another team.

5. Test these batteries to confirm or deny the results of the first team.

6. Exchange with one more team and test its batteries in the same way.

CONDUCTORS AND INSULATORS

A material conducts electricity if it is added or substituted within a working electric circuit and the bulb remains lit.

Directions:

1. Gather as many pieces of different materials as you can to test if they will conduct electricity.

   _____ small pieces of dry cloth

   _____ small pieces of dry paper, such as tissue or paper towel

   _____ plastic pen caps

   _____ metal pieces of pens

   _____ wood ruler with metal edge

   _____ pencil lead

   _____ scissors

   _____ binder clips

   _____ clamps

   _____ wet tissue or paper towel

   _____ small piece of wet cloth

   _____ crayon

   _____ dry leaves

   _____ damp leaves

   _____ eraser

   _____ plastic protractor

   _____ metal protractor

   _____ chalk

   _____ marker

   _____ _____

   _____ _____

   _____ _____

   _____ _____

   _____ _____

   _____ _____

2. Use your completed circuit apparatus from Activity 1.

3. Disconnect one of the wires attached to the battery. Attach a third wire (with $1\frac{1}{2}$ inches of insulation removed from both ends) to the battery.

4. To test if a material will conduct electricity, touch the two loose wires (one from battery, one from light) to the material. The bulb will light if the material does conduct electricity.

5. Test as many of the materials above as you can. Mark a **Y** next to it if the material kept the circuit open and **N** if the circuit was closed and the light did not go on. Put an **S** if it barely lit or lit for a brief moment.

6. How would you describe a nonconductor of electricity?

   _____

   _____

   _____

NAME _____

CONDUCTORS AND INSULATORS

HOW MANY LIGHTS ON ONE BATTERY

Directions: Do this activity with 2 or 3 teams.

1. Hook up one complete circuit as before.

2. Work with one other team and share their light bulb and socket apparatus.

3. Attach the second bulb and socket to yours by connecting it to your socket apparatus with a wire from one flange of your socket to one of theirs and connect the other wire to the remaining flange.

4. If it lights, determine if both lights are as bright as they were before. If it doesn't light, reverse the wires on the flanges or hook the wires directly to the battery in the same way the first socket is connected.

5. If the second light also works, try hooking the socket from a third team in the same way.

6. Try to get as many lights working off one battery as you can.

7. Illustrate your light bulb and battery arrangement below.

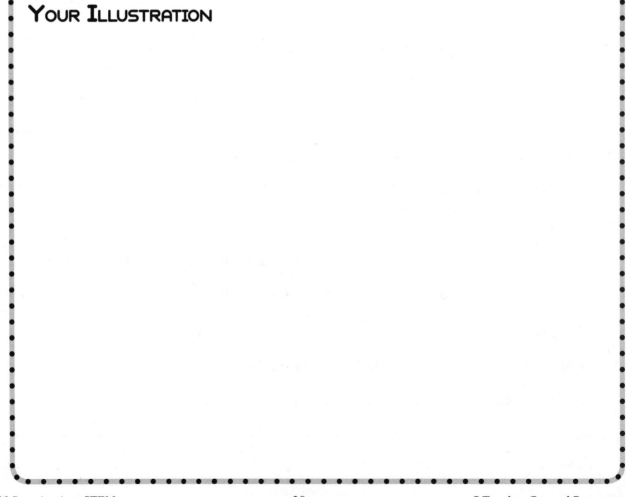

YOUR ILLUSTRATION

CONDUCTORS AND INSULATORS

JOURNAL ENTRY

1. Describe the results from the battery-testing activity. How many batteries did you find were still working? How many dead batteries did you discover? Which batteries were hardest to test? Why?

_____

_____

_____

_____

_____

2. Which materials did you discover would conduct electricity? Which materials would not conduct electricity?

_____

_____

_____

_____

_____

3. Could a damp piece of paper towel take the place of a wire to connect a socket to a battery? How could you test it? Would the paper towel work if it was rolled tight like a wire? Would the paper towel work if it was soft? How would you find the answer?

_____

_____

_____

_____

_____

DESIGN PROCESS REVIEW—CONDUCTORS AND INSULATORS

Share the investigations in this activity and your responses in the Journal Entry in a classroom discussion with your fellow classroom scientists.

MAKING A LIGHT-BULB TELEGRAPH

Directions: Work in teams of two as you perform this activity. Gather these materials as directed by your teacher.

TEAM MATERIALS

- 2 large paper clips or 2 pieces of thin metal
- 2 pieces of coarse sandpaper cut into 2-inch-by-2-inch squares
- aluminum foil
- D cell batteries

- D cell battery holders of any type or large rubber bands
- flashlight bulbs and sockets
- scissors and a ruler
- thin bell wire (22 gauge works well)

NOTE: If you use small C, AAA, or AA batteries in a large plastic battery holder, use a spongy wad of aluminum foil to fill out the rest of the space in the battery holder and keep the paper clips or metal flanges upright and next to the batteries or aluminum foil.

GETTING STARTED

1. A light-bulb telegraph uses the same basic materials and arrangement as a complete circuit.

2. Use a battery holder or two large rubber bands to tightly hold the battery. Firmly place the metal flanges or large paper clips in the holder or between the battery and the rubber bands on both metal poles of the battery.

3. Screw the small flashlight bulb securely into the socket.

4. Attach 1 wire to one large paper clip or flange on one side of the battery. Make sure there is metal-to-metal contact between the paper clip or flange and the bare end of the wire. Attach the other bare end of the wire to one metal flange on the socket.

5. Attach one bare end of the remaining wire to the other flange of the socket.

6. Wrap another large paper clip securely with the other bare end of this wire. This will be the telegraph key used to tap coded messages. Touch the paper clip to the flange to get the light bulb to light up.

The telegraph model looks like this:

MAKING A LIGHT-BULB TELEGRAPH

SENDING MESSAGES

This is the code used to send messages on a telegraph.

INTERNATIONAL MORSE CODE

A • –	G – – •	M – –	S • • •	Y – • – –	4 • • • • –
B – • • •	H • • • •	N – •	T –	Z – – • •	5 • • • • •
C – • – •	I • •	O – – –	U • • –	0 – – – – –	6 – • • • •
D – • •	J • – – –	P • – – •	V • • • –	1 • – – – –	7 – – • • •
E •	K – • –	Q – – • –	W • – –	2 • • – – –	8 – – – • •
F • • – •	L • – • •	R • – •	X – • • –	3 • • • – –	9 – – – – •

A telegraph sends messages using a combination of dots and dashes. On this model, a dot is a 1 count and a dash is a 2 count. You should count to <u>three</u> between letters. Count to <u>four</u> between words. Count to <u>five</u> between sentences.

Compose three messages on the lines below. Translate them into Morse code.

1. Message _____

   Code _____

2. Message _____

   Code _____

3. Message _____

   Code _____

Choose one of the messages to send to a partner by using your telegraph. Send it carefully using the instructions on the previous page by holding the paper clip to the empty flange for the appropriate counts. Give your partner time to decode the message using his/her code page.

When you have finished sending, your partner will use his or her telegraph to send a message to you.

Message from first partner

Code: _____

Translated: _____

Switch roles and send and receive another message.

Message from second partner

Code: _____

Translated: _____

MAKING A LIGHT-BULB TELEGRAPH

JOURNAL ENTRY

1. What did you learn about how telegraphs work by doing this project?

    _____

    _____

    _____

2. Which letters or numbers of the code did you learn to use by memory? What made them easier to learn?

    _____

    _____

    _____

3. Explain why a light-bulb telegraph might be easier to work with in a classroom than the telegraphs that click.

    _____

    _____

    _____

4. How might you use your study of electric circuits in other ways at home or at school?

    _____

    _____

    _____

5. Which letters are probably the most used letters in the English language? How could you learn the answer from this activity?

    _____

    _____

    _____

DESIGN PROCESS REVIEW—LIGHT-BULB TELEGRAPH

Share your experiences and the information you learned with your classmates in a discussion led by your teacher.

 <u>_____</u>

TESTING TELEGRAPHS

CHALLENGE ACTIVITY—MULTIPLE CIRCUITS

Challenge Assignment: Hook up and use as many telegraph sets as you can. Send the same message over several or all of the telegraph sets. You may choose to use the Design Process Worksheet on page 5 to help you.

Materials: Telegraph model units from the last activity

1. Each team should hook up their telegraph model as they did in the last activity.
   A. The battery is in the battery holder or held firmly by strong rubber bands—usually doubled over to firmly hold the battery and paper clip.
   B. A large paper clip is held against each pole of the battery by the rubber bands.
   C. A 6-inch wire (bare at each end) is attached to one end of the large paper clip.
   D. A 6-inch wire (bare at each end) is attached to the other large paper clip.
   E. One end of one wire is attached to the metal flange of the socket.
   F. The other bare end of the other wire is wound firmly to one more large paper clip.

   NOTE: This paper clip is the telegraph key used to send messages by tapping the code on the other flange of the socket. This paper clip is also the easiest way to attach two telegraph sets (by hooking it to the empty side of the socket).

   Below is an example of how you could attach telegraph sets.

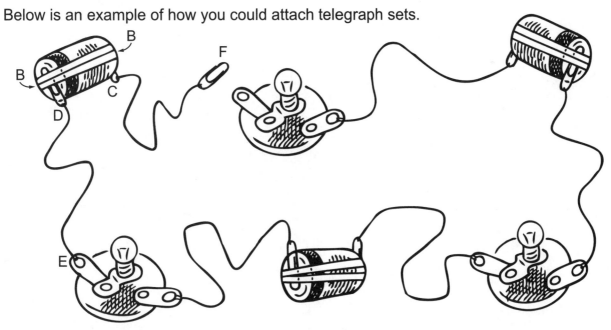

2. Send a short message on the assembled telegraphs you have. As needed, tighten any connections on your equipment.

3. Work together with multiple teams so that your assembled machines are connected and working smoothly.

4. Create a message to send on your equipment. Use the Morse code on page 31 to write and send your message.

N A M E _____

TESTING TELEGRAPHS

CHALLENGE ACTIVITY—THE GREAT HOOK-UP

Talk with other teams and see how many different ways you can hook up your telegraph units.

Carefully hook up each telegraph unit and then check it by sending a message.

If one bulb doesn't light . . .

1. Check each connection.

2. Make sure each bulb is screwed tightly in its socket.

3. Make sure each battery is firmly attached.

4. Make sure all wires are in contact with the socket and the battery.

Use your remaining time to try different types of connections that keep your telegraph unit working well. How many different ways could you connect the sets?

Illustrate some of the connections below.

 _____

TESTING TELEGRAPHS

CHALLENGE ACTIVITY—JOURNAL ENTRY

Use a computer, tablet, or other device to answer each paragraph subject below. Use complete sentences and describe your experiences clearly.

PARAGRAPH 1

How well did your "Great Telegraph Hook-Up" work? How many sets did you connect? Did all of the sets stay in operation? What interesting things happened during this experiment?

What other discoveries did you make in using these hook-ups?

PARAGRAPH 2

What would you do next time if you did the telegraph hook-up again? How would you organize it? How many sets would you use? What would you do differently?

PARAGRAPH 3

Respond to these questions by referring back to the activities you completed in this unit.

1. *How do you make a complete circuit?*

2. *How do you make and use a model telegraph?*

3. *How do you make and use multiple circuits?*

4. *How can you send and receive messages on a telegraph?*

5. *How does a telegraph really work?*

DESIGN PROCESS REVIEW—TESTING TELEGRAPHS

Share your investigation and experiences with your classmates in the class discussion your teacher leads to culminate this unit.

AIR AND WATER

4 Sessions: 1 session per each activity (approximately 1 to $1\frac{1}{2}$ hours per session)

CONNECTIONS & SUGGESTIONS

SCIENCE—Evaporation is a natural process by which liquid water is converted to gas. The regular movement of water through the liquid and gas state helps cleanse it of impurities and allows its constant replenishment on Earth in an endless cycle of movement from clouds to precipitation. The conversion of gas to liquid is called *condensation*. Students can see this condensation on a container holding cold water or ice.

Water molecules diffuse in a liquid (or gas) medium. This diffusion of molecules is demonstrated in the second activity when the food coloring spreads through the clear water in the bottle.

Air pressure increases when it is heated. Air is not as accurate for measuring temperature as the mercury in a thermometer, of course, but the effect of heat on pressure is the same. The expanding air pushes down on the colored water that then rises in the straw, giving an indication of higher temperatures. The temperature increase is measured in centimeters in this activity.

TECHNOLOGY—The materials and apparatus used in the experiment constitute one technology application. Students will use basic computer software to write a brief report in which they describe the activities done during the project and to record results of various investigations.

ENGINEERING—Students will use a variety of engineering designs and materials in the lesson in order to create an apparatus for working with evaporation and condensation. They will develop tools to enhance and illustrate diffusion of molecules, temperature measurement, and how atomizers work.

MATH—Students will use rulers to measure temperature variations in metric terms. Students will also work with angles.

Materials
- baggies
- chalk dust
- clear plastic cups
- clear plastic straws
- eyedroppers
- flour
- food coloring

- hot water
- ice
- individual water bottles
- jar tops, lids, or small plates
- jars
- modeling clay
- plastic or paper bowls

- protractors
- rulers
- stiff paper or tagboard
- tap water
- thermometers (optional)
- water glasses

For Challenge activity:
- fishing line
- magnifying glass
- mirrors

- plastic-coated bowls/plates/cups
- salt and pepper
- tape

- thin straws/flex straws
- thin wire
- very large straws

· · · · UNIT 2 VOCABULARY · · · ·

atom—the basic building block of solids, liquids, and gases; it can exist on its own or it can combine to form molecules

atomizer—an apparatus for reducing liquids to a fine spray

condensation—the change from a gas to a liquid produced by a change of temperature

diffusion—the dispersion of particles through a gas (such as air) or a liquid (such as water)

evaporation—the change of a liquid to a gas; occurs with water or other liquids

molecules—the smallest particles of water (or other substances) that have all the properties of that substance

precipitation—the condensation of water falling as rain or snow

temperature—the measurement or intensity of heat in a liquid, gas, or solid

three states of matter—solid, liquid, and gas

DISCUSSION PROMPT:

When a region receives consistently below-average precipitation for an extended period of time, it is considered a drought. Droughts can persist for a few months or even years. Some areas of the world have annual dry seasons that can increase the chances of drought and of subsequent damage from heat and fires. Often, human activities can contribute to drought conditions by negatively impacting the ability of land to capture and hold water. What do you think some of these human activities are? How do you think evaporation and condensation figure into drought conditions? What are some ways that people can use their knowledge of evaporation and condensation in order to conserve water?

WATER, WATER, ALL AROUND

Evaporation is the changing of a liquid to a gas. *Condensation* is the change of a vapor into a liquid or solid. Both of these are components in the water cycle, also known as the hydrologic cycle. Water is always changing states in a continuous movement on, above, and below the surface of the Earth. It takes form as liquid, vapor, and ice, and the process of changing states can take place very quickly or over thousands of years.

Ocean saltwater makes up over 96% of Earth's water, while freshwater makes up only a little over 2%. When the sun heats up water in the oceans or rivers or lakes, some of the water turns to vapor or steam (evaporates) and goes into the air. Some water vapor also goes into the air from plants when they lose water out of their leaves. This is called *transpiration*. What is it called when people lose water from their bodies (i.e. sweat)? Perspiration! Evaporation, transpiration, and perspiration are all acts that involve water changing to vapor and going into the air. (The salts and other, heavier materials are left behind.) You will be creating an atomizer in this unit, which is a device that will create a mist from a liquid. In essence, you will be conducting an experiment that is vaporizing the liquid, similar to condensation in the water cycle.

Once water vapor rises higher in the air, it cools down and changes back into liquid form, creating clouds. This is the act of condensation. You can witness this type of change at home, too. For example, if you pour cold water into a glass on a hot day, you'll notice that water droplets start forming on the outside of the glass. It's not water leaking out of the glass, it's water vapor from the air. When it touches the cold glass, it changes back into a liquid. When you make your own cloud in the first activity, you will experience condensation first hand.

Diffusion is the movement or spreading out of molecules (or atoms) from an area of high concentration to low concentration. In the thermometer activity, you will watch how this happens in water and study its effects. You will also study how air pressure affects water and its temperature. There are many different components that affect the water cycle!

Use a computer or tablet to search for information on the Internet to help you as you complete the activities in this unit. Helpful search terms include:

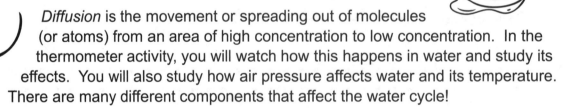

condensation	water cycle	clouds
evaporation	temperature	thermometer
diffusion	atomizer	

MAKE YOUR OWN CLOUD

GETTING STARTED

Weather is a critical element of life on Earth, and the behavior of water in its three states—solid, liquid, and gas—is a basic part of Earth's many weather features.

Directions: Work in teams of two as you perform your first activity. Gather these materials as directed by your teacher.

TEAM MATERIALS
- baggies
- chalk dust
- flour
- hot water
- ice
- jar tops or lids (or small plates)
- jars or water glasses

1. Fill a glass jar or a water glass about $\frac{1}{3}$ full of hot water.

2. Sprinkle some chalk dust, flour, or both in the air above the hot water.

3. Cover the glass or jar with an upside-down lid or plate.

4. Place a baggie with ice cubes on top of the upside-down lid or plate.

5. Observe what occurs in the jar or glass.

6. Describe the cloud that forms. How much of the space in the jar does it fill?

   _____

   _____

   _____

7. What do you think happened to form the cloud?

   _____

   _____

   _____

8. What conditions in the atmosphere do you think are necessary to create clouds?

   _____

   _____

   _____

MAKE YOUR OWN CLOUD

9. What do you often see when you open a freezer door on a warm day?

_____

_____

_____

10. What gradually happened to the cloud you created in the jar?

_____

_____

_____

11. What forms on the lid or plate holding the ice? The term for these drops of water is *condensation*. Where else did the condensation form?

_____

_____

_____

12. Place your bag of partially melted ice cubes in a warm place such as an outdoor table, on the blacktop, or on cement on a warm day. Watch how the condensation forms. Describe what happens. How long did it take?

_____

_____

_____

13. How long did it take for the ice to become water? How long did it take for the water to become warm or to match the temperature of the outside air?

_____

_____

_____

MAKE YOUR OWN CLOUD

JOURNAL ENTRY

Describe what you learned in the experiment. What natural events have you seen that involve condensation?

_____

_____

_____

When have you felt some condensation on your body? What weather conditions cause some condensation?

_____

_____

_____

What appliances cause condensation to form on your skin? How?

_____

_____

_____

What appliances help remove condensation from your skin?

_____

_____

_____

What natural events remove condensation from your skin?

_____

_____

_____

DESIGN PROCESS REVIEW—MAKING YOUR OWN CLOUD

Share the experiment and your Journal Entry responses with your classmates in a class discussion led by your teacher.

NAME

BOTTLE THERMOMETER

Directions: Work in teams of two as you perform this activity. Gather these materials as directed by your teacher. This activity should be performed on a warm day.

TEAM MATERIALS
- clear plastic straws
- eyedroppers
- food coloring
- individual water bottles
- modeling clay
- ruler
- stiff paper or tag board
- thermometer (optional)
- water

GETTING STARTED

1. Fill a 16-ounce water bottle $\frac{1}{2}$ full with clear tap water.

2. Use the eyedropper to carefully place 2 drops of food coloring into the water in the bottle.

3. **Don't shake the bottle.** Use a watch or clock to time the diffusion of molecules within the bottle.

4. Record what happens to the water after the times listed below.

   1 minute: _____

   _____

   2 minutes: _____

   _____

   3 minutes: _____

   _____

   4 minutes: _____

   _____

   _____

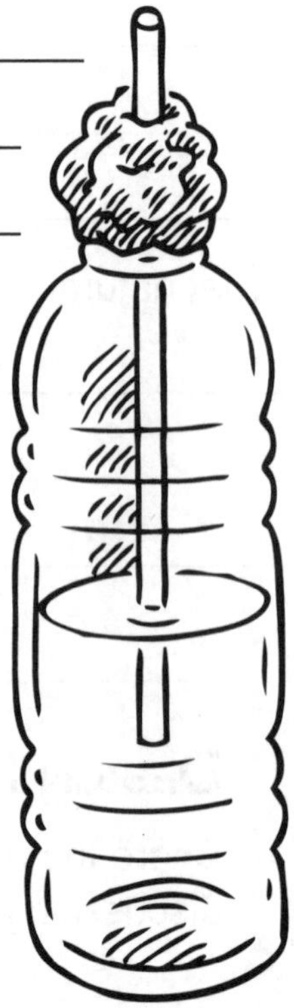

MAKING THE THERMOMETER

1. Wrap about 1 ounce of modeling clay around the straw $1\frac{1}{2}$–2 inches from the end of the straw, as shown in the illustration on the right. Be sure to keep the straw open. Stick the straw into the water bottle. Make sure the straw sticks at least 1 inch into the water. Wrap the clay holding the straw tightly around the mouth of the bottle so that no air can escape from the bottle—except from the straw.

 NAME _____

BOTTLE THERMOMETER

MAKING THE THERMOMETER *(cont.)*

2. Make a measuring strip using a thin piece of stiff paper or tag board about 10 inches long and 1 inch wide.

3. Using the metric side of the ruler, mark the stiff paper at the centimeter lines. Number them 1 to 25. The measuring stick should extend from the water level to the end of the straw.

4. Double-check your clay seal at the top of the bottle.

5. Find a warm place to set your thermometer outside the room. Choose a sunny place, a warm patio table, a cement or blacktop surface in the sun, a metal table, or a similar place.

6. Check your temperatures every 15 or 20 minutes throughout the day. Record the temperatures below. (Optional: Use a mercury thermometer if available to record the temperature in Fahrenheit or Centigrade/Celsius degrees.)

TIME	HEIGHT OF THE WATER IN THE STRAW	TEMPERATURE F° OR C°

7. How many centimeters did the water rise during the day? _____

8. What was the last temperature in terms of centimeters? _____

9. About how many degrees on a regular thermometer did one centimeter above the water level in the bottle equal? _____

BOTTLE THERMOMETER

JOURNAL ENTRY

1. Why do you think mercury is used in a thermometer rather than water?

   _____

   _____

2. How does the water bottle thermometer indicate that the temperature is rising?

   _____

   _____

3. What happens to the water in the bottle on a very hot day?

   _____

   _____

4. What is forcing the water to rise in the straw?

   _____

   _____

5. What do you think is happening to the air in the bottle when the bottle is sitting in the hot sun?

   _____

   _____

6. Why would the bottle thermometer not work if there were leaks in the clay? What would happen to the heated air?

   _____

   _____

DESIGN PROCESS REVIEW—BOTTLE THERMOMETER

Share the experiment and your experiences with your classmates in a discussion led by your teacher. Be sure to refer to your Journal Entry responses.

 **N A M E** _____

 **N A M E** _____

ATOMIZERS

Directions: Work in teams of two as you perform this activity. Gather these materials as directed by your teacher.

NOTE: Do this activity outside on a warm day.

TEAM MATERIALS
- clear plastic cups
- protractors
- straws
- water

You Need to Know: This activity is based on Bernoulli's Principle, a scientific discovery by Daniel Bernoulli in the 1700s that proved that when air is in motion, its pressure is reduced. The more rapid the motion of air, the greater the reduction in pressure. Anything that the air is moving over will be inclined to rise in response to the lower pressure.

MAKING AN ATOMIZER

An atomizer is a device that draws a liquid up by changing the air pressure above it from a higher pressure to a lower pressure. An atomizer creates a fine mist that is a combination of water and air molecules. A perfume dispenser is often an atomizer. A good video demonstration of a straw atomizer can be found at ***https://www.youtube.com/watch?v=-Q5KjBlgiHU***

Directions:

1. Fill a clear plastic cup about $\frac{3}{4}$ full of water.

2. Place and hold a straight straw in the water straight up in the water. Do not rest the bottom of the straw against the bottom of the glass.

3. Hold a clean straw next to the top of the first upright straw at about a 90-degree angle as shown in the illustration. Blow through this second straw so that the air goes across the top of the first straw.

4. Observe what happens to the water in the upright straw and in the cup.

5. Do several trials until your atomizer works well.

ATOMIZERS

6. Try holding the straw at different angles when you blow into it in order to see which will give you the best results. Do 3 trials at each angle. Record your best results at each angle. Start by refilling your cup until it is about $\frac{3}{4}$ full again. For the angles that worked well, indicate with a **W**. For those that didn't work, indicate with **DW**.

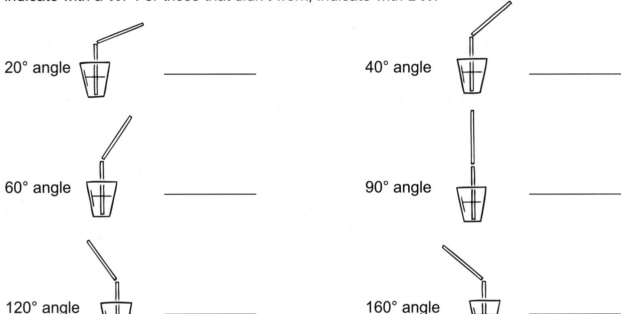

20° angle _____   40° angle _____

60° angle _____   90° angle _____

120° angle _____   160° angle _____

7. Refill the cup. Try using a flex straw in the cup. Arrange the flex of the straw in a variety of angles. Blow across the open end of the flex straw. Illustrate the angles that worked well.

Angles That Worked Well

1.   2.   3.   4.

8. Arrange the straw in the glass so it is straight up again. Make sure you raise the straw in the water so that it is not sitting on the bottom. Hold the half straw at a 90-degree angle and blow as hard and as fast as you can across the top of the first straw.

9. What can you determine about the atomizer based on the speed or strength with which you blow?

_____

_____

_____

10. Does more or less water spray from the top of the flex straw in the water? _____

ATOMIZERS

JOURNAL ENTRY

1. Which angle worked best for your atomizer? How could you tell?

   _____

   _____

   _____

2. What other materials might have worked very well for your atomizer? What kinds of straws, tubes, or other equipment would have worked well?

   _____

   _____

   _____

3. Could you get this atomizer to work in a strong windstorm? How would you arrange the materials?

   _____

   _____

   _____

4. What do you think happens when a high wind blows across a river, a lake, or an ocean? Describe what you think could occur.

   _____

   _____

   _____

5. Could you get the atomizer to work with just one straw by blowing across the cup of water?

   _____

   _____

   _____

DESIGN PROCESS REVIEW—ATOMIZERS

Share your observations, ideas, experiences, and suggestions with your class during the discussion led by your teacher.

 **NAME** _____

WATER, AIR, WIND, AND HEAT

CHALLENGE ACTIVITY—INVENTION

You have just learned about temperature's effect on evaporation, condensation, and pressure and the effect of wind moving over water. Use this knowledge to create your own invention.

You may combine two or three different concepts or just create your own bigger, smaller, better, or more interesting version of a thermometer, atomizer, or cloud machine.

You may want to combine two or more ideas, such as using a water bottle thermometer and the cloud. You may wish to use a bag of ice to affect any of the experiments you design.

Use the Design Process Worksheet on page 5 to help guide you through the invention process.

REMEMBER: Your invention may simply be a different or improved design feature on something the class did. For example, it might involve very large straws, flex straws, or very thin straws for several different models, a magnifying glass or mirrors for condensation or evaporation, large plastic bottles for several different activities, thin wire or fishing line for attaching materials, different kinds of tape, and paper- or plastic-coated plates.

SOME SUGGESTED MATERIALS:

- fishing line
- ice
- magnifying glasses
- mirrors
- pepper/salt/flour
- plastic bottles (large or small)

- plastic-coated bowls/plates/cups
- tape
- thin straws, flex straws
- thin wire
- very large straws
- water

 NAME _____

WATER, AIR, WIND, AND HEAT

CHALLENGE ACTIVITY—INVENTION *(cont.)*

Work with a partner and brainstorm several ideas. Write them down on your Design Process Sheet. List the ideas that you think may work. On the lines below, list the materials you will need to have and who will be responsible for bringing them.

_____

_____

Your Invention Idea—Sketch:

Describe your invention and its purpose or function.

_____

_____

_____

Explain how to assemble your invention.

1. _____

_____

2. _____

_____

3. _____

_____

4. _____

_____

5. _____

_____

6. _____

_____

Test your invention and evaluate it. List the test results and modifications on your Design Process Worksheet.

WATER, AIR, WIND, AND HEAT

CHALLENGE ACTIVITY—INVENTION *(cont.)*

Below are some ideas for inventions that you may try if you're not sure where to begin.

SUGGESTION # 1

Create an atomizer using a squiggly or twisted straw. Set the straw in a cup of water. Try blowing across the squiggly straw with your regular half straw that you used in earlier activities. Observe the water in the squiggly or twisted straw as it rises and sprays.

What is different about this atomizer? Does anything change the flow of water? Does it look different?

_____

_____

_____

SUGGESTION # 2

Create a water-bottle atomizer. Fill a plastic water bottle to the rim. Try using a long plastic straw to blow across the top of the bottle. See how much of the bottle you can empty using your breath.

How many centimeters of water did you remove with your atomizers?

_____

SUGGESTION #3 *(Do this outside)*

Cover a paper plate with a very thin layer of water from an atomizer. Place one small drop of red food coloring in one section of the plate. Place one small drop of another color in a second section of the plate. Place one small drop of a different color in a third section of the plate. Leave the plate undisturbed for the color to diffuse and the water to evaporate.

Examine the plate when it is completely dry.

Describe the appearance of the plate. How did the color spread? What happened as evaporation occurred?

_____

_____

_____

WATER, AIR, WIND, AND HEAT

CHALLENGE ACTIVITY—JOURNAL ENTRY

Use a computer, tablet, or other device to answer each paragraph subject below. Use complete sentences and describe your experiences clearly.

PARAGRAPH 1

What was the original plan of your invention as you and your partner designed it?

How did the plan change? Why did it change?

PARAGRAPH 2

What problems did you encounter in making the invention? Describe the problems and your solutions.

PARAGRAPH 3

What did you learn about air and water in doing this unit? Give specific details.

PARAGRAPH 4

Respond to these questions by referring back to the activities you completed in this unit.

1. *How do clouds form?*

2. *What causes evaporation and condensation?*

3. *How do molecules of water diffuse in a solution?*

4. *How does a thermometer work?*

5. *How does an atomizer work?*

DESIGN PROCESS REVIEW—WATER, AIR, WIND, AND HEAT

Share your invention and experiences with your classmates in the class discussion/presentations your teacher leads to culminate this unit.

REFLECTION AND REFRACTION

4 Sessions: 1 session per each activity (approximately 1 to $1\frac{1}{2}$ hours per session)

CONNECTIONS AND SUGGESTIONS

SCIENCE—Students will explore the angle of reflection and the angle of incidence, and they will experiment with different ways light causes reflection.

TECHNOLOGY—Students will assemble and use various pieces of equipment that are part of the technology in use. Students will use basic computer software to write a brief report on the project, describing the problems encountered, the solutions attempted, the success rate of each activity, different approaches used, and suggestions for improvement.

ENGINEERING—Students will use the materials listed in the lesson to create an apparatus for working with reflection and refraction. Students will experiment with a variety of engineering designs and the listed materials to create various combinations of equipment to test their scientific hypotheses.

MATH—Students will use protractors to determine the angles needed for each mirror activity and to determine angles of reflection and refraction.

Materials

- aluminum foil
- chalk
- clear plastic cups (preferred)
- colored markers
- cooking oil
- diffraction gratings (optional)
- dish soap
- eyedroppers
- flashlights
- index cards
- liquid soap

- magnifying glasses
- masking tape
- paper clips, small and large
- paper money
- paper towels
- pencil/pen/marker
- pennies (200)
- photo
- print alphabet
- prisms
- protractors

- rulers, yardsticks, or measuring tape
- scissors
- small mirrors
- spray bottle
- thin straws and regular drinking straws
- transparent plastic
- water
- white paper

UNIT 3 VOCABULARY

<u>mirror</u>—a shiny metal, glass, or plastic object that reflects light

<u>prism</u>—a triangular piece of glass or other clear material that slows down the speed of light and shows the seven colors of the spectrum

<u>reflection</u>—the sending back of an image using a mirror or shiny object

<u>refraction</u>—the bending of a wave of light as it moves from one medium to another such as from air to water

<u>spectrum</u>—a series of colored bands separated and arranged by their wavelengths as light passes through a prism or an object, such as water, that refracts light

<u>white light</u>—light composed of a spectrum of seven visible colors: red, orange, yellow, green, blue, indigo, and violet

DISCUSSION PROMPT:

When looking into a regular mirror, the image reflected back to you is a fairly good representation of what you look like. In curved mirrors, however, such as funhouse mirrors, the reflection is distorted so that you can look a lot taller or shorter than you normally would. If you look at yourself in a **concave** (curved inward) mirror, you will look a lot larger, if you look at yourself in a **convex** (curved outward) mirror, you will look smaller. What do you think you would look like if you saw yourself in a funhouse mirror that had both concave and convex portions?

REFLECTION AND REFRACTION

A mirror is a smooth surface such as glass or shiny metal that forms images by reflecting light. A ray of light striking a mirror reflects light back at the same angle at which the light struck the mirror. The angle at which a ray of light strikes an object is called the *angle of incidence*. The angle that reflects light back is called the *angle of reflection*. The angle of incidence equals the angle of reflection. Therefore, a ray of light striking a mirror at 30° (the angle of incidence) equals the angle at which it is reflected back (the angle of reflection).

Holding two mirrors at right angles to each other creates two reflected images of objects in front of the mirrors. The images are laterally inverted, which means that the right side of the object appears as the left side of the reflection. The image of the reflection appears as the same shape as the object being reflected.

Some shapes have one line of symmetry, such as the capital letter **H**. The two sides of the **H** have the same size and shape, but they are mirror images of each other. You could fold the shape over exactly on top of itself. Placing a mirror along a line of symmetry of such an object illustrates the symmetry because the mirror image completes the shape. Using a mirror helps illustrate whether an object is truly symmetrical or not. It is especially useful in working with geometric figures.

Refraction is the bending of light caused when light travels through certain substances. When light travels from one transparent substance to a denser transparent substance—from air through water or glass, for example—it travels more slowly; this tends to cause light to bend or refract. How much the light bends depends on the substance through which it is traveling and the angle at which the light is hitting the substance through which it is traveling.

For example, when light is traveling part of the way through air and part of the way through water (as with a straw stuck in a glass of water), the light reflecting from underwater comes from a different angle than the light from the part of the straw above water. The object therefore appears broken or bent at the water line. This bending of light below water also tends to have a magnifying effect, making the straw appear larger than it is.

Light from sunlight, a lamp, or a flashlight is called white light. White light is composed of the seven colors of the spectrum: red, orange, yellow, green, blue, indigo, and violet. Each color of light refracts or bends at a slightly different angle, splitting light into these seven colors. A prism is an object that refracts light. Many prisms are triangular in shape and made of clear glass, plastic, or quartz. These seven colors are easily seen when light shines through a prism. Water is a natural prism that splits light into a band of colored lights. A rainbow is a spectrum caused by falling drops of water through which the sun is shining.

Use a computer or tablet to search for information on the Internet to help you as you complete the activities in this unit. Helpful search terms include:

reflection	refraction	symmetry
angle of reflection	angle of incidence	prism

MIRROR MUSINGS

REFLECTION

Directions: Work in teams of two as you perform your first activity. Gather these materials as directed by your teacher.

> ### TEAM MATERIALS
>
> - aluminum foil
> - masking tape
> - scissors
> - small hand mirrors
> - yardstick, measuring tape, or rulers
>
> **NOTE ABOUT MATERIALS:** If mirrors are not available in sufficient quantities for students to each have one, carefully cut aluminum foil pieces about 4 inches by 4 inches and tape them (with the shiny side out) to pieces of cardboard or stiff folder material about 3 inches by 3 inches. Masking tape on the back of the card will hold the foil firmly in place.
>
> Students will need to be more careful about bending the materials than they would with metal or glass mirrors.

GETTING STARTED

With a partner, tape a hand mirror about head high to a wall or board. Use masking tape on the back of the mirror or along the edge, if necessary. Next, tape a yardstick, measuring tape, or rulers in a straight line on the floor directly below the mirror.

1. Stand with your partner about 6 inches from the mirror on the wall. Look in the mirror. Can either of you be seen from where you are standing?

   _____

   Can both of you be seen? _____

2. Move 1 foot farther away from the mirror. Can either of you be seen from where you are standing?

   _____

   Can both of you be seen? _____

3. Move 1 more foot farther from the mirror.

   Can either of you be seen from where you are standing?

   _____

   Can both of you be seen? _____

4. Measure the distance at which both of you can be seen in the mirror together.

   Record the feet and inches: _____ feet _____ inches

5. To be seen together, did you need to be closer to or further from the mirror?

   _____

NAME _____

MIRROR MUSINGS

ANGLE OF INCIDENCE AND ANGLE OF REFLECTION

Directions: Work in teams of two as you perform this activity. Gather these materials as directed by your teacher.

> ### TEAM MATERIALS
> - books
> - mirror
> - paper clip
> - paper money
> - paper or plastic cups
> - pencil/pen/marker
> - penny
> - photo
> - protractor
> - ruler
> - scissors
> - shoe
> - string

1. Hold the pencil straight up and down in the middle of the mirror. Use the protractor to make sure it forms a right triangle in the mirror.

   Observe the reflection. What angle does the reflection show? _____

   _____

   _____

2. Change the angle of the pencil. Observe the reflection. Use the protractor to measure the

   angle of the pencil: _____

   What is the angle of reflection shown in the mirror? _____

A FUNDAMENTAL LAW OF SCIENCE:

The Angle of Incidence (the angle of the pencil) equals The Angle of Reflection (angle in the mirror).

3. Hold the pencil at several different angles. Does the reflection always equal the angle of the pencil?

   _____

4. Which direction does the reflection point compared to the pencil?

   _____

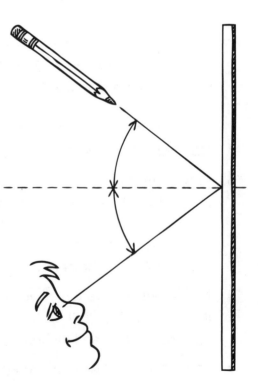

 NAME _____

MIRROR MUSINGS

ANGLE OF INCIDENCE AND ANGLE OF REFLECTION (cont.)

5. Use each of the items you collected and observe the reflections. List each item and record anything remarkable or unusual that occurs as you do this activity. Use your protractor to record each angle.

Item	Angle	Comments
_____	_____	_____
_____	_____	_____
_____	_____	_____
_____	_____	_____
_____	_____	_____
_____	_____	_____
_____	_____	_____

6. Place a penny so that you can see both sides of the coin in the mirror at the same time. At what angle did you have to hold the penny? _____

7. Illustrate the penny and the reflections in the mirror in the box below.

8. Arrange a book so that you can see the front of the book, the back of the book, and the spine of the book at the same time.

   Illustrate the book and mirror reflection below.

 NAME _____

MIRROR MUSINGS

HINGED MIRRORS

Directions: Work in teams of two as you perform this activity. Gather these materials as directed by your teacher.

TEAM MATERIALS

- aluminum foil
- large paper clips
- masking tape
- pennies, other coins
- protractors (one for each team)
- rulers
- scissors
- small metal hand mirrors (or other small mirrors)

TEACHER: Collect enough metal or glass hand mirrors so that each team of students has two similar mirrors. If you use aluminum foil mirrors, make sure the foil is unwrinkled and tight against the cardboard backing.

GETTING STARTED

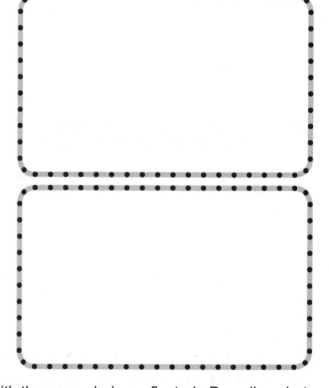

1. Place two mirrors side by side. Use two or three strips of masking tape to connect the mirrors **on the back** so they will open and close like a book. Sketch your setup in the box.

2. Open the two mirrors so that they form a straight line. This is a 180-degree straight angle. Place one penny on the desk at the center where the two mirrors meet. You should see the penny reflected—half on one mirror and half on the other mirror. Sketch your setup in the box.

3. Compare the penny in the mirror reflection with the penny being reflected. Describe what is the same and what is different.

   _____

   _____

   _____

4. Slowly move the two mirrors in so that they form about a 120-degree angle. Use a protractor to help you get the 120-degree angle. How many pennies can you now see reflected in the mirrors? _____

MIRROR MUSINGS

HINGED MIRRORS *(cont.)*

5. Move the mirrors so that they form exactly a 90-degree (right) angle.   Use the protractor to check the degrees. Place the penny on the desk where the two mirrors meet. Sketch your setup in the box.

How many pennies can you now see reflected in the mirrors? _____

6. Move the mirrors closer to about 80 degrees. Can you see 5 pennies? _____

In which direction is the head of the penny facing? _____

7. Arrange the mirrors to get the most pennies to show.

How many pennies can you see, including the real penny? _____

What is the angle formed by the two mirrors? _____

8. What happens to the penny reflections when you get to an angle of 40 or 45 degrees?

_____

_____

9. Do the same activity with a large paper clip. What is the most paper clips you can see with the mirrors including the real paper clip? _____

10. At what angle do you see the most paper clips? _____

11. Why is the total image that you see always an odd number of paper clips (or pennies)?

_____

MIRROR MUSINGS

JOURNAL ENTRY

1. What was the most interesting observation you made about mirrors today? Describe what you saw.

_____

_____

_____

2. Explain the fundamental science law of reflection. Describe how it works.

_____

_____

_____

3. What is meant by the "angle of incidence"?

_____

_____

_____

4. Describe what you observed about reflections with two mirrors at different angles.

_____

_____

_____

5. Which experiments would have been especially interesting with a door-sized bedroom mirror? How would they work with a large hand-held mirror?

_____

_____

_____

DESIGN PROCESS REVIEW—MIRROR MUSINGS

Share your observations with your fellow students in a classroom discussion led by your teacher.

 NAME _____

SYMMETRY

ALPHABET REFLECTION

Directions: Work in teams of two as you perform this activity. Gather these materials as directed by your teacher.

> **MATERIALS**
> • hand mirrors   • index cards   • print alphabet (capital letters)   • white paper

1. Study the list of the capital letters of the alphabet below.

A B C D E F G H I J K L M N O P Q R S T U V W X Y Z

2. Make a list of the letters you think are exactly symmetrical—one side of the letter is exactly equal to the other side.

    Symmetrical Letters: _____

3. Use a mirror and a printed copy of the letters to check your list. You can print a copy on separate index cards. Place the **A** card on your desk. Place your mirror at a right angle down the center of the letter top to bottom. Does the mirror create the entire letter exactly as it should look? _____

    Is the capital **A** a symmetrical letter? _____

4. Use the same procedure to check the remaining letters and list the vertically symmetrical printed letters below.

    Vertically symmetrical capital letters: _____

    What other kind of symmetry can you see in some of the letters? _____

    _____

5. Look at the list of letters above. Lay the mirror along the capital letter E horizontally at the middle line of the E.

    Is this letter horizontally symmetrical? _____

6. Check each letter again with the mirror to see which other letters are horizontally symmetrical. List them below.

    Horizontally symmetrical capital letters: _____

7. What do the printed letters **H, I, O,** and **X** appear to have in common? What symmetry do they illustrate?

    _____

    _____

    _____

SYMMETRY

SYMMETRY IN THE CLASSROOM AND BEYOND

There are a number of things in the classroom and on the playground or school campus that can reflect either vertical or horizontal symmetry when a mirror is used near them. For example, the structure of a math textbook, a football, a basketball, or a box of crayons can show symmetry.

Use your mirror to test different classroom items. Make a list of materials that can be tested and found symmetrical in shape and those which are asymmetrical (not the same shape on both sides). Check boards, desks, tiles, art materials, and other equipment.

Symmetrical Items	Asymmetrical Items
_____	_____
_____	_____
_____	_____
_____	_____
_____	_____
_____	_____
_____	_____

LIVING SYMMETRY

Some living or once-living creatures also demonstrate vertical symmetry. Use your mirror to check blades of grass, seeds, shells, fossils, and tracks. You may also notice symmetry in a classroom pet or a friend. Use the mirror for the inanimate objects and (with permission) check a friend's ears, nose, eyebrows, hands, and general appearance for symmetry.

Ways living things are symmetrical or almost symmetrical:

_____

_____

_____

Ways living things are not symmetrical or nearly symmetrical:

_____

_____

_____

 NAME _____

SYMMETRY

SWITCH IT UP

Why doesn't a mirror show symmetry with some palindromes such as **R E D D E R** or **R A D A R** or **M A D A M**?

_____

_____

Can you make up a word (real or not) that will show symmetry in a mirror such as **H U H** or **M A T T A M**? Explain your answer.

_____

_____

What type of letters would have to be used in the middle of a five-letter word?

_____

What type of letters would have to be used at the beginning and end of the word?

_____

The great artist and scientist Leonardo Da Vinci often wrote left-handed and backwards in his native Italian language. This was probably because he was naturally left-handed and he also didn't want some powerful people to be able to understand his scientific ideas. He was able to easily read his notes by using a mirror.

Try printing 3 sentences—either **right-handed or left-handed**—and **backwards**.

1. _____

2. _____

3. _____

Then try reading them with a mirror.

Switch sentences with a partner or friend. Use a mirror to decode their sentences.

Switch #1 _____

_____

Switch #2 _____

_____

Switch #3 _____

_____

SYMMETRY

JOURNAL ENTRY

What scientific information about mirrors did you learn today?

_____

_____

_____

How could you apply what you learned today in class or at home?

_____

_____

_____

What would you like to learn about mirrors, reflection, and light?

_____

_____

_____

Why were the two mirrors so interesting when hooked together?

_____

_____

_____

What experiment would you like to do with the two mirrors that you didn't get to do or finish?

_____

_____

_____

DESIGN PROCESS REVIEW—SYMMETRY

Share your experiments and experiences with the class in a discussion moderated by your teacher.

NAME _____

REFRACTION

OBSERVING REFRACTION IN WATER

Directions: Work in teams of two as you perform this activity. Gather these materials as directed by your teacher.

> **TEAM MATERIALS**
> - clear plastic cups
> - colored markers
> - diffraction gratings (optional)
> - eyedroppers
> - flashlights
> - magnifying glasses
> - mirrors
> - pencil, pen, or thin stick
> - prisms
> - protractors
> - regular drinking straws with some color
> - spray bottle
> - water
> - white index cards or white paper

1. Fill a clean, clear plastic cup about $\frac{3}{4}$ full of water. Place a regular drinking straw in the water at about a 30-degree angle.

2. Observe the appearance of the straw from above. Move it in different directions and observe the straw several times from above. What do you see?

   _____

   _____

3. Get down at eye level with the cup of water and the straw. What appears to have happened

   to the straw? _____

   _____

4. Move the straw in different directions. Does it still appear bent? _____

5. Put the straw in the clear cup of water as shown here: Light traveling through the water is slowed down, causing the straw to appear bent. Look at your protractor. At what angle does the straw appear to be bent?

   _____

6. Hold the straw straight up and down in the water. What is different about this direction?

   _____

7. Is the straw pointing straight down? _____

8. What has happened to the appearance of the straw where it is sticking in the water?

   _____

   _____

NAME _____

REFRACTION

MORE REFRACTION

1. Place a pencil, pen, crayon, or thin stick into the water. What changes about the

   appearance of the item you used? _____

   _____

2. Does the changed appearance show from the top or only from the sides? _____

   _____

NATURE'S PRISM

Directions:

1. Fill the clear plastic cup about $\frac{2}{3}$ full of water. Place a small glass or metal mirror at a slant in the cup. Put the cup in the full sunlight. Position the cup so that the sun is shining in through the water. (Use a flashlight to shine through the water if the sun is not bright.)

2. Find where the spectrum is showing on the walls, floor, or outdoor table. It's best to do this activity near light-colored walls and floors.

3. Position a plain white index card or white sheet of paper on the wall or table where the spectrum of color is showing. You should see some or all the colors of the rainbow refracted through the water onto the white paper.

4. Use markers to record the bands of color that are created when the light hits the water. Recreate what you saw in the space below.

5. Spray (or observe as your teacher sprays) water from a spray bottle into the direct sunlight. Spray in several different directions to determine where the rainbow is most pronounced.

 NAME _____

REFRACTION

TRY THIS

1. Dip the magnifying glass into the cup of water. Remove the wet glass with drops still on the glass. Hold the glass in the direction of the sun.

   Describe what you see. In the box, draw a sketch of what you see.

   _____

   _____

   _____

   _____

   _____

   _____

   _____

2. Hold the dropper with water facing the sun. Hold a white card or paper behind the dropper so that you see the dropper and then the paper. What do you see? Were you able to see the spectrum against the white card? In the box, draw a sketch of what you see.

   _____

   _____

   _____

   _____

   _____

   _____

   _____

REFRACTION

USING A GLASS OR PLASTIC PRISM

Prisms effectively demonstrate how light can be refracted. Shining sunlight, a flashlight, or another source of white light through the triangular glass or plastic quickly presents a spectrum of the seven colors that compose white light: red, orange, yellow, green, blue, indigo, and violet. Isaac Newton made one of the fundamental discoveries of modern physics when he shined a light through a prism and realized that light is composed of these 7 colors and that they each have different angles of refraction.

Use prisms to study the refraction of sunlight or any other source of light. Experiment with the light sources and measure the width of each color refracted through the prism. Record your results below.

REFRACTION CHART	
COLOR	WIDTH

DIFFRACTION GRATINGS

A diffraction grating is a piece of treated plastic that breaks light into its component colors. It is similar to a prism, except the color shows on the grating itself. If you have some of these plastic gratings from an old science kit, hold them up to the sunlight or even classroom light and notice the varied colors that show on the plastic.

Draw what you see. Include the various shades of color, the position and shapes the colors make, and anything that you observe with the light and the grating.

REFRACTION

JOURNAL ENTRY

1. Which of the activities you did today dealt with the fact that water is a natural magnifier (because it refracts light)?

   _____

   _____

   _____

2. Which ways did you make a rainbow today?

   _____

   _____

   _____

3. Which colors of the spectrum (the rainbow) did you see today in doing the experiments?

   _____

   _____

   _____

4. Does light slow down or speed up when it passes from air to water?

   _____

   _____

   _____

5. How can you tell different colors of the spectrum are slowed at different rates of speed when light passes through water?

   _____

   _____

   _____

DESIGN PROCESS REVIEW—REFRACTION

Share your experiences and experiments with the class in a discussion led by your teacher.
Listen for the different experiences of your classmates.

 NAME _____

CREATE YOUR OWN LIGHT EVENT

CHALLENGE ACTIVITY—INVESTIGATING LIGHT

Challenge Assignment: Conduct an investigation on light and its properties by completing one of the activities on the following pages or by creating an investigation of your own. You may use the Design Process Worksheet on page 5 to help you.

Directions:

1. You may utilize any of the materials you and your partner used while doing this unit, including: mirrors, clear plastic cups, flashlights, magnifying glasses, aluminum foil, coins, prisms, paper clips, etc. You might also consider using small pieces of transparent plastic, soap, or cooking oil.

2. You may want to work with another team and combine supplies, but stick to one objective—one plan of discovery. Everyone on the team should agree to follow the investigation to the end.

3. **Very important:** Follow through on your plan until you have found that something does or does not work.

4. **Scientists keep records. Record the results of the investigation as you go.** Write down what happens on your Design Process Worksheet. (Everyone needs to keep their own records.)

5. Start with an idea to test.

6. Write down the plan for the test.

> *Remember:* **What doesn't work teaches scientists and students just as much as what does work.**

Be efficient. Use your time well.

If you finish early, continue the plan. Add more components. Retest some parts of the experiment.

NOTE: The next pages give some starting ideas and procedures for possible explorations for those students unsure where to start. They are not complete lessons. You have to follow through.

CREATE YOUR OWN LIGHT EVENT

CHALLENGE ACTIVITY—SUGGESTED INVESTIGATION #1

Lesson Topic Question: What can you discover about reflection and/or refraction using a clear cup of water, two mirrors, a flashlight, and small classroom objects such as pencils, straws, crayons, a magnifying glass, and masking tape or clear packing tape?

Question to Be Investigated: How will two mirrors in a cup of water refract light or reflect objects?

1. Assemble the materials listed above. Sketch your setup in the box.

2. Place the clear cup of water on the desk about $\frac{2}{3}$ or $\frac{3}{4}$ full. You don't want the water spilling out.

3. Use a piece of masking tape or sticky plastic packing tape to connect the mirrors edge-to-edge.

4. Place one straw in the cup. Adjust it different ways.

5. What did you observe? _____

_____

6. Use these materials in the cup and record what you observed. Rearrange the materials as needed.

Straws _____

Pencil _____

Crayon _____

Other object _____

7. Remove the objects. Add the magnifying glass. Continue on your own from here.

 NAME _____

CREATE YOUR OWN LIGHT EVENT

CHALLENGE ACTIVITY—SUGGESTED INVESTIGATION #1 *(cont.)*

Observations and Tests:

Write down observations you made for each round of testing.

Test 1:

_____

_____

_____

Results:

_____

_____

_____

Test 2:

_____

_____

_____

Results:

_____

_____

_____

Test 3:

_____

_____

_____

Results:

_____

_____

_____

CREATE YOUR OWN LIGHT EVENT

CHALLENGE ACTIVITY—SUGGESTED INVESTIGATION #2

Topic # 1: How will one dropper ($\frac{1}{2}$ full of dish soap) affect reflection and refraction in a cup of water with 1 mirror and with 2 mirrors?

Topic #2: How will one dropper ($\frac{1}{2}$ full of cooking oil) affect reflection and refraction in one cup of water with 1 mirror and 2 mirrors?

GETTING STARTED

1. Place 1 mirror in the cup of water. Fill an eyedropper about $\frac{1}{2}$ full of dish soap by squeezing the bulb at the top of the eyedropper and then letting go. Squeeze the dropper of soap into the water. Stir the water slightly if bubbles don't form right away. Sketch your setup in the box.

2. How are the bubbles reflected in the mirror inside the cup? Describe the size, colors, and movement of the bubbles.

   _____

   _____

3. Add the second mirror to the cup. Describe what you see in the double mirrors.

   _____

4. Fill the eyedropper $\frac{1}{2}$ full of cooking oil and release the oil into the water. Describe the colors created in the solution and the behavior of the oil and water as seen in the mirrors.

   _____

   _____

5. Slowly stir the solution with the dropper. Observe and record what is reflected in the mirrors.

   _____

   _____

   Continue and record your tests and observations below:

   _____

   Tests (What you did)

   _____

   _____

   Observations

   _____

   _____

CREATE YOUR OWN LIGHT EVENT

CHALLENGE ACTIVITY—YOUR OWN TEAM INVESTIGATION

Clearly State the Investigation Your Team Will Do:

_____

_____

_____

Test You Will Conduct (Step-by-step Procedures):

_____

_____

_____

_____

Materials Needed:

_____

_____

What You Think Will Happen:

_____

_____

Observations:

_____

_____

_____

_____

Results of Test:

_____

_____

_____

CREATE YOUR OWN LIGHT EVENT

CHALLENGE ACTIVITY—JOURNAL ENTRY

Use a computer, tablet, or other device to respond to each paragraph subject below. Use complete sentences and describe your experiences clearly.

PARAGRAPH 1

What was the intent of each investigation you planned? How did you set up the investigations?

PARAGRAPH 2

What didn't turn out as expected? Why? What went wrong? What would you do differently next time?

PARAGRAPH 3

What did you learn from each investigation?

PARAGRAPH 4

What did you learn about light, mirrors, and reflection in doing this unit?

PARAGRAPH 5

Respond to these questions by referring back to the activities you completed in this unit.

1. *How can you use mirrors to produce multiple reflections of an object?*

2. *What is the nature of a reflected image compared to the original object?*

3. *How can you refract light with water?*

4. *What is a spectrum, and how can you produce one?*

5. *What are the angle of incidence and the angle of reflection?*

DESIGN PROCESS REVIEW—INVESTIGATING LIGHT

Share your tests, results, experiences, and observations with other teams during the class discussion your teacher leads to culminate this unit.

 **UNIT 4**

WATER PRESSURE AND CAPILLARITY

4 Sessions: 1 session per each activity (approximately 1 to 1$\frac{1}{2}$ hours per session)

CONNECTIONS AND SUGGESTIONS

SCIENCE—Students will explore the properties of water, capillary action, and how a siphon functions.

TECHNOLOGY—The materials and equipment used in this activity are part of the technology component. Calculators are used to compute amounts of water lifted. Computers are employed to record information and to summarize results.

ENGINEERING—The engineering for most siphons is quite simple. Sucking out the air from a straw is, of course, the simplest way to make a siphon. The formation of other siphons involves specific engineering arrangements for tubing to allow water to flow uphill.

MATH—Knowing the amount of water moved and the distance it travels involves measurement and learning terms related to volume and comparisons of liquid measurement.

Materials

- books or blocks of wood
- clear plastic or paper cups (about 100)
- clear, thin plastic or rubber tubing (about 24 inches per team)
- colored pencils
- flat pans or plastic tubs for water
- flex straws (about 60)
- food coloring (optional)
- measuring cups
- paper towels of various types

- regular plastic straws
- rubber bands
- rulers
- scissors
- thin straw, stirrer, or wooden barbecue skewer
- thin wire (22 gauge or so)
- tissue
- washable colored markers
- water

For Challenge activity:

- black electrical tape
- cups of various sizes/pails

- various pieces of hose

UNIT 4 VOCABULARY

atmospheric pressure—the force exerted by the weight of air in the atmosphere of Earth

atom—the basic building block of solids, liquids, and gases that can exist on its own or combine to form molecules

capillarity—the process by which liquids contained in a very thin tube (as thin as a hair) or absorbant material rise or fall as the result of surface tension

continuous siphon—a long siphon that continues to function until the source of water is removed

molecule—a particle made up of atoms that is held together by chemical bonds

siphon—a tube or pipe for moving water or other liquids

self-starting siphon—a siphon that can be induced to start by its design and location

surface tension of water—the tendency of molecules of water to adhere, or stick, to each other

water pressure—the force exerted by water against any object or material contained within it

DISCUSSION PROMPT:

Did you know that there are animals that have their own siphons? Different types of mollusks, including some sea snails, clams, and even octopuses have them. Their siphons are used to "smell" or "taste" the water in order to hunt for food. Some animals use their siphons to intake water for locomotion and respiration. Some even use them as a snorkel to breathe underwater! If you had a siphon attached to you, what do you think you would use it for?

WATER PRESSURE AND CAPILLARITY

Siphons are common tools used for moving water from a lower place to a higher one. They work for several reasons. When air is removed from a tube, water (or other liquid) will rush in to take its place as long as the tube is empty and the water source is available. Water will even flow uphill against the force of gravity in the vacuum created by the removal of the air.

Water seeks its own level. This is why a siphon can be used to fill an empty cup to the same level as the water left in the original cup.

Capillary action is the force working in a paper siphon. Molecules of water are not only attracted to each other but also to the tube-like spaces between the molecules of paper in the paper towel. Water will climb these paper towel tubes and move along the towel to the next cup. Water will also climb along the spaces in a paper towel to the top where it gradually evaporates into the air. Capillary action works best with higher quality/thicker paper towels in which the tubes are smaller and the paper is woven more tightly.

When a person sucks on a straw, they are actually removing the air from the straw, causing the liquid in the cup to move up the straw and to fill the vacuum.

The siphons in these activities work because gravity pulls the water out of the lower end of the siphon. Liquid always flows from an area of higher pressure to one of lower pressure. Atmospheric pressure pulls the water up the tube, and gravity pulls it down and out the bottom.

Liquid in the container flows up the tube towards an area of lower atmospheric pressure, then flows out the tube because of gravity. This lowers the pressure again and pulls more water into the tube and then out. Atmospheric pressure is essential to the operation of a simple siphon. The cup of water that is being emptied must be open to the air so that air pressure pushes down on the water in the cup and keeps the siphon working.

Use a computer or tablet to search for information on the Internet to help you as you complete the activities in this unit. Helpful search terms include:

> capillarity   water pressure   siphon
>
> surface tension   reservoir

SIPHONS

MAKING A SIMPLE SIPHON

Directions: Work in teams of two as your perform your first activity. Gather these materials as directed by your teacher.

> ### TEAM MATERIALS
> - 2-foot-long clear flexible tubing pieces
> - 6- or 8-ounce clear plastic cups
> - flat pans or plastic tubs for water
> - measuring cups
>
> - regular and flex plastic straws
> - scissors
> - water

GETTING STARTED

1. Place a regular drinking straw all the way in a cup full of water. Place your finger firmly over the top of the straw. Lift the straw, keeping your finger firmly covering the top of the straw. Hold the straw over an empty measuring cup and release your finger from the top of the straw. How much water did you place into the empty measuring cup?

_____

2. Do the activity again. Hold the straw at different angles in the cup. Does it work every time? When does it work best? Do some angles work better than others?

_____

_____

3. Try using a flex straw to do the same activity. Does this straw hold as much water or more water?

_____

4. Manipulate the straw using the flex part of the straw in the water. Can you get the straw to hold more water, or does it hold the same amount? What did you do?

_____

_____

_____

_____

5. Draw a sketch in the box to the right showing the setup that allowed the most water to be held in the straw.

NAME _____

SIPHONS

MAKING A TUBE SIPHON

Directions:

1. With a partner, fill two 8-ounce plastic cups $\frac{1}{2}$ full of water. Select a piece of clear or white plastic tubing 2 feet in length. Lay the tubing flat in a pan of water. Observe the bubbles of air coming out of the ends of the tubing.

2. Once the tube is full of water, cover both ends firmly with your thumbs or forefingers. Keep the ends covered and insert one end into each cup. Remove your thumbs or forefingers when the tube ends are in the water or on the bottom of the cup. Keep the tube below the water level and lift one cup 2 or 3 inches. Observe the results. Fill the tube again and get the cups $\frac{1}{2}$ full again. Lift the one cup again and lower it. Do the same with the other cup. Describe what happened and draw a sketch of your setup in the box.

_____

_____

SIPHONS

MAKING A TUBE SIPHON *(cont.)*

3. Use the 2-foot-long tubing again. With your partner, set up a continuous siphon by lifting one cup and tube end and then the other cup and tube end to keep the water flowing back-and-forth between the cups.

4. How long were you able to keep the continuous siphon going before one of the cups emptied and you had to refill the cup and start again?

_____

5. What problems did you encounter using the tubing to keep the continuous siphon going?

_____

_____

6. Would larger cups have worked better? Why?

_____

_____

7. Sketch your setup in the box below.

 NAME _____

SIPHONS

CONTINUOUS SIPHON

Directions:

1. Create a continuous siphon using just three flex straws. Make a slit in the edge of the short flex end of a straw and fit the slit end into the longer end of another flex straw.

   Make a slit in the short end of a third flex straw and fit it inside the long end of the first straw.

2. Fill two cups $\frac{2}{3}$ full of water. Lay the straw siphon in the tub of water until it is full of water. Cover the ends with your thumbs or forefingers. Set one end of the siphon in each cup below the water level and uncover the siphon ends.

   Do several trials or work with a partner until you have the siphon working smoothly as you lift and lower the cups.

3. Describe your results.

   _____

   _____

   _____

4. How much water were you able to move from one cup to the other?

   _____

5. Did you entirely empty one cup of water and siphon it all into the other cup?

   _____

6. Can you set up a continuous siphon with the three straws so that the water is moving from one cup to another or back-and-forth? How did you do it? Sketch your setup in the box to the right.

   _____

   _____

   _____

   _____

SIPHONS

JOURNAL ENTRY

1. Where have you seen a siphon in operation at home, at school, or someplace else?

   _____

   _____

   _____

2. Why would a siphon be useful in an aquarium, fish tank or bowl?

   _____

   _____

   _____

3. What happens to a siphon when the container runs out of water?

   _____

   _____

   _____

4. Which was the easiest siphon to use? Why?

   _____

   _____

   _____

5. What could you personally use a siphon for at home or in a science class?

   _____

   _____

   _____

DESIGN PROCESS REVIEW—SIPHONS

Share your Journal Entry responses and experiences with your class in a discussion moderated by your teacher.

PAPER TOWEL SIPHONS

Directions: Work in teams of two as you perform this activity. Gather these materials as directed by your teacher.

TEAM MATERIALS

- book or block of wood
- clear plastic cups
- colored pencils
- different types of paper towels and tissues
- food coloring (optional)
- thin straw, stirrer, or wooden barbecue stirrer
- washable colored markers
- water

SETTING UP

1. Fill a clear plastic cup with water to about one centimeter from the top. Place it on a table or desk. Carefully twist one paper towel into a thin, tight roll. Stick one end of the paper towel roll into the full cup of water and the other end into an empty cup. Observe what happens. What were the results? How long did it take to fill the second cup half full? Make a sketch showing what happened.

_____

_____

2. Lift the first cup about 1 or 2 inches and set it on a book or a block of wood. Does the siphon keep working? Did the siphon empty the first cup?

_____

_____

3. Reverse the cups so that the second cup is on the block of wood or book and the first one is on the desk. Does the siphon refill the first cup? Describe what happens.

_____

PAPER TOWEL SIPHONS

SETTING UP *(cont.)*

4. Make a new paper towel siphon. Place a few drops of food coloring on the middle of the siphon or use a washable marker to color a 1-inch-wide mark down the center of the siphon. Place the siphon in the water, and be careful not to submerge the colored mark in the middle. Keep the full cup higher than the second cup. What happens to the water and the siphon?

_____

_____

_____

5. Which cup begins to receive the colored water? Why? Using markers or colored pencils, sketch what happened to the colored mark that is on the paper towel in the box below.

_____

_____

_____

PAPER TOWEL SIPHONS

1. Work with a partner to set up this activity. Try two or three different types of paper towels and/or tissues for your siphons. Set up pairs of cups with a regular paper towel, a school classroom paper towel, and a tissue. Remember to twist each paper as tightly as possible. Try to start each siphon at the same time. Observe the results.

   Which siphon started working first? _____

   Which siphon was the slowest? _____

   Which siphon moved the most water? _____

   Which siphon emptied the cup first? _____

   Illustrate your
   siphons here:

2. This tissue paper siphon can be effective but messier than the other siphons. Try doing this version:

   Twist the tissue as thin and tight as possible. Feed the tissue into a flex straw. (Use a very thin straw, stirrer, or wood barbeque skewer to **gently** push the tissue through the flex straw.) Place one end of the tissue in a straw into a half-cup of water. Bend the other end and place it into an empty cup. Time how long it takes to move the water into the empty cup. Record your results. Make sure the water cup is higher than the empty cup.

3. Try another kind of siphon with paper or cloth. Illustrate your paper or cloth siphon here:

4. Rank your siphons below from best (#1) to worst (#5).

   1. _____

   2. _____

   3. _____

   4. _____

   5. _____

 _____

PAPER TOWEL SIPHONS

JOURNAL ENTRY

1. Which was your most successful siphon? Why do you think it was successful?

    _____

    _____

    _____

2. Which siphon surprised you the most because it worked? Why?

    _____

    _____

    _____

3. Where have you seen a siphon working at home?

    _____

    _____

    _____

4. What siphon do you use every day? Explain your answer.

    _____

    _____

    _____

5. How could you get water out of a glass if you couldn't touch or lift the glass or use a straw?

    _____

    _____

    _____

DESIGN PROCESS REVIEW—PAPER TOWEL SIPHONS

Share your Journal Entry responses and other observations with your class during the class discussion led by your teacher.

SELF-STARTING SIPHONS

Directions: (This activity requires patience and several trials. You may wish to view this video on self-starting siphons to help you: *https://www.youtube.com/watch?v=4SEv_GxAo70*) Work in teams of two as you perform this activity. Gather these materials as directed by your teacher.

> **TEAM MATERIALS**
> - clear plastic cups
> - clear plastic tubing (aquarium tubing works well)
> - rubber bands and/or thin wire
> - water

1. Use about 18 inches (1 $\frac{1}{2}$ feet) to 2 feet of clear plastic tubing for this siphon. Use thin bell wire or rubber bands to make two curves at one end, as shown in the illustration. Make sure the first curve in the tubing is lower than the second. (If you use a rubber band, you will need to use wire for the other tie, as you couldn't slip another rubber band over the first curve.)

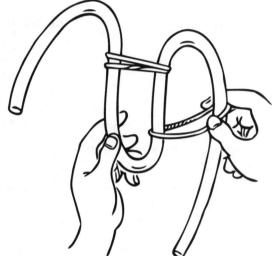

2. Place the curved end of the self-starting siphon slowly in a full cup of water so that the tube fills with water. Place the other end of the tube in an empty cup. (You may need to jiggle the curved end slightly.)

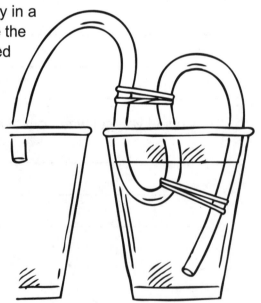

3. How much water from the first cup flowed through the self-starting siphon into the second cup? Did it empty or half-empty the first cup?

_____

_____

SELF-STARTING SIPHONS

IMPROVING RESULTS

1. Use the same self-starting siphon tube from the previous activity. Fill the first cup of water again. Elevate this cup by sitting it on a block of wood or a higher surface such as a step. Put the empty cup below, and start the siphon by putting it into the cup of water—curved-loop end first. Sketch your setup in the box below.

2. Describe what happened.

   _____

   _____

   _____

3. How much water came out of the first cup? _____

4. How long did it take once it got started? _____

5. How many trials or attempts did it take to get this siphon to work? What did you have to do to get the siphon to work? Did you have to jiggle or adjust the curved loop?

   _____

   _____

   _____

   _____

   _____

   _____

   _____

SELF-STARTING SIPHONS

REVERSE THE SIPHON

1. Reverse the position of the siphon from the activity above so that the curved loop of the siphon is in the lower cup full of water. Jiggle the curved portion of the siphon. Can you get the water to go uphill? Describe what happened. Sketch the results.

_____

_____

2. Set up an arrangement like the one illustrated below with the siphon elevated in the middle about 1 inch above both cups. Can you get the siphon to work? Jiggle the first end. Start with a level siphon and then elevate the tube in the middle. Record your results.

RESULTS: _____

_____

_____

_____

_____

3. Using the same arrangement described above, elevate the middle of the siphon to see how high you can get it and still get the siphon to function. Describe your efforts and results. How many inches or centimeters were you able to elevate the center of the siphon?

_____

_____

_____

 _____

SELF-STARTING SIPHONS

JOURNAL ENTRY

1. In a children's book named *Henry Reed's Babysitting Service* by Keith Robertson, a rather clueless teenager left a hose with one end dangling in the swimming pool and the other end hanging down the open window into the cellar below the house. What do you think happened?

    _____

    _____

    _____

2. How would the hose serve as a siphon to empty the pool into the cellar? Why would the hose be full of water?

    _____

    _____

    _____

3. Why did the pool have to be higher than the cellar for the hose to serve as a siphon?

    _____

    _____

    _____

4. How far into the pool would the hose need to be to empty the pool?

    _____

    _____

    _____

5. What did you learn to do in this activity? How could you use this information?

    _____

    _____

    _____

DESIGN PROCESS REVIEW—SELF-STARTING SIPHONS

Share the investigations in this activity and the responses in your Journal Entry in a classroom discussion led by your teacher.

 NAME _____

SUPER SIPHONS

CHALLENGE ACTIVITY—CREATE YOUR OWN SUPER SIPHON

Challenge Assignment: Using your knowledge from the previous investigations, create your own super siphon to move as much water as possible from one cup to another. You may choose to assemble the siphons in either of the suggested activities listed, or create your own. Make sure you use the Design Process Worksheet on page 5 to record your investigation.

MATERIALS

- black electrician's tape
- cups of various sizes, pails
- rubber bands
- thin wire
- tubing of various lengths and diameters
- various pieces of hose
- water
- water tray, plastic food-storage container, or bussing tray from a restaurant

SUGGESTED ACTIVITY #1

1. On a tray, assemble 4 cups of various sizes or 4 large cups. Find 3 pieces of tubing of various lengths—between $1\frac{1}{2}$ and 2 feet (18 to 24 inches) long.

2. Fill the cups with water to different heights—such as $\frac{1}{4}$, $\frac{1}{2}$ full, $\frac{3}{4}$, and nearly full.

3. Assemble the tubing between the 4 cups by placing the tubing in the pan of water to replace the air, holding your fingers at each end of the tubing, and placing the tube with one end in each of 2 cups.

4. Do the same procedure with each of the two remaining tubes. Remember: the water must replace the air, and don't release your fingers or thumbs from the tube's opening until it is in the water.

5. Now that you have the siphon working, try to keep it functioning by lifting and lowering cups to keep the water flowing back and forth among the cups.

6. Add a fourth piece of tubing to connect the cups in a circle.

7. Try to keep the four-cup siphon working by raising and lowering cups and adjusting the tubing. Time how long you can keep this system going before one cup empties and the system stops.

   Sketch your setup in the box below.

 N A M E _____

SUPER SIPHONS

CHALLENGE ACTIVITY—CREATE YOUR OWN SUPER SIPHON (cont.)

SUGGESTED ACTIVITY #2

MATERIALS
- 8 cups of the same size
- markers
- paper towels of various kinds
- watch or clock
- water

1. Twist four pieces of paper towel into 4 long twists or folds about 8 inches (20 centimeters) long. Mark one end of each paper towel with a band of bright color from a marker.

2. Fill four cups of the same size (8 ounce or larger) with water up to 2 centimeters from the top. Place four empty cups of the same size about 4 inches from the first four cups. Sketch your setup in the box.

3. Start each siphon at the same time from the full cup. (Each partner can start two at a time.)

4. Time each siphon until the first drop hits the bottom of the empty cup. Record the number of minutes and seconds.

5. Time each siphon until the first cup is empty.

6. Complete the table below to show the comparisons.

SIPHON TABLE			
COLOR	PAPER TOWEL NAME	FIRST DROP	FIRST EMPTY CUP

 NAME _____

SUPER SIPHONS

CHALLENGE ACTIVITY—CREATE YOUR OWN SUPER SIPHON *(cont.)*

CREATE YOUR OWN SIPHON ACTIVITY

1. What do you want to test, experiment with, or prove in your activity?

    _____

    _____

2. What do you think will be the result of your experiment?

    _____

    _____

3. List your materials needed:

    _____

    _____

4. How will you do the test or experiment? List the steps below:

    a. _____

    b. _____

    c. _____

    d. _____

    e. _____

5. What were your results?

    _____

    _____

    _____

    _____

    In the box below, draw a sketch of your siphon.

SUPER SIPHONS

CHALLENGE ACTIVITY—JOURNAL ENTRY

Use a computer, tablet, or other device to respond to the paragraph topics below. Use complete sentences and describe your experiences clearly.

PARAGRAPH 1

What were you trying to accomplish, test, prove, or disprove in this activity?

PARAGRAPH 2

What did you learn about siphons in this activity?

PARAGRAPH 3

Which siphon experiment done by any team in your class most impressed you? Why?

PARAGRAPH 4

What could you use a siphon for at home?

PARAGRAPH 5

Respond to these questions by referring back to the activities you completed in this unit.

1. *What does a siphon do, and how is it made?*

2. *What materials can you use to make a siphon?*

3. *How can you make a self-starting siphon?*

4. *How does a siphon function?*

5. *When do people use a siphon?*

DESIGN PROCESS REVIEW—SUPER SIPHONS

Share your investigation, observations, experiments, and conclusions with your classmates in the class discussion your teacher leads to culminate this unit.

MAGNETISM AND ELECTROMAGNETISM

4 Sessions: 1 session per each activity (approximately 1 to 1½ hours per session)

CONNECTIONS AND SUGGESTIONS

SCIENCE—Students will explore the force of magnetism, magnetic poles, and electromagnetism creating a magnetic field through the application of electricity.

TECHNOLOGY—Students build apparatuses to test magnetic force, use magnets, and make temporary magnets as part of the technology of the project. Students will use basic computer software to write a brief report on the project, describing the problems encountered, the solutions attempted, the success rate of each activity, different approaches used, and suggestions for improvement.

ENGINEERING—Students will use the materials listed in the lesson to create apparatuses for working with magnets and electromagnets. Students will experiment with a variety of engineering designs and the listed materials to create various functioning combinations of equipment to test their scientific hypotheses.

MATH—Students will use rulers to determine the distances that each type of magnet will be able to attract a metal object in selected activities.

Materials

- batteries (C, D, AA, or AAA)
- battery holder or large thick rubber bands
- books
- Bristol board or similar material
- fishing line (8 lb. test or stronger is best)
- index cards
- iron filings
- magnets (any type)
- manila folder or piece of tag board
- nails (various sizes—uncoated)
- needles/pins
- paper clips

- paper plates
- rulers
- scissors
- small disk or rectangular magnets
- small metal objects
- tape
- thin coated wire, a small piece of sandpaper, aluminum foil
- thin, flexible metal strips about 1 to 2 centimeters wide and about 30 centimeters long (or longer) (metal report holders and clamps work well)

NOTE TO THE TEACHER: *There are many places such as the Internet or a dollar store to get an inexpensive supply of classroom magnets that are used in these activities. Small round or square ceramic magnets will work for these activities.*

UNIT 5 VOCABULARY

attraction—a tendency to pull towards; opposite poles of a magnet attract

electromagnet—a magnet created by running a current of electricity around a piece of iron

induction—the process of creating a magnet—for example, a temporary magnet can be created by friction when a piece of metal is rubbed in one direction

iron filings—small metal shavings removed from a piece of iron

magnetic—having the power to attract certain metal objects

permanent magnet—a magnet that retains its magnetic properties

repulsion—a tendency to push away; like poles of a magnet repel

temporary magnet—a magnet created by induction or electricity that does not retain its magnetic influence

magnetic pole—a point at either end of a magnet where the magnetic force is the strongest

DISCUSSION PROMPT:

Earth has its own magnetic field. This field extends from Earth's core all the way out into space, where it meets the solar wind, which is a stream of particles coming from the Sun. The magnetic field deflects these particles, protecting the ozone layer. What do you think would happen if Earth suddenly lost its magnetic field? Can you think of other important magnets that are used to keep things on Earth running smoothly and safely?

MAGNETS

Magnets have remarkable properties. They attract and are attracted by specific metals such as iron, nickel, and cobalt. They are usually made from metal elements, or alloys. Magnets have north and south poles. Magnets produce magnetic fields, and magnetic lines of force leave a magnet from its north pole and enter through a magnet's south pole. Opposite poles attract—the north pole of one magnet is attracted to the south pole of another magnet. Like poles repel each other—two south poles repel each other and so do two north poles.

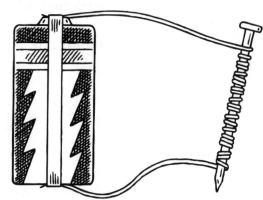

Permanent magnets create their own magnetic fields all the time. Temporary magnets produce a magnetic field for a short time while in the presence of a magnetic field. The field soon leaves after the temporary magnet is removed from the magnet's magnetic field. Magnetic and electrical fields are related in that a current of electricity in a coil wrapped around a steel nail can create an electromagnet. Magnetism is one of the four fundamental forces in the universe, along with gravity (and strong and weak atomic forces).

Iron and a few other similar materials possess tiny magnetic domains with a north and south pole. In a normal piece of non-magnetic iron, these domains are pointing every which way, in no organized manner. In a magnet, however, these domains are all aligned with the north poles pointing in the same direction. This is the same thing that happens when a piece of metal such as a needle or nail is magnetized by rubbing the object in one direction. The domains line up for a time.

A compass needle is a permanent magnet that is attracted to the north magnetic pole on Earth. Magnets are even used by cattle farmers to keep cows from accidentally swallowing chunks of iron, nails, nuts, and other metal objects.

Use a computer or tablet to search for information on the Internet to help you as you complete the activities in this unit. Helpful search terms include:

magnets	electromagnets	magnetic fields	electromagnetic fields
particles	magnetic force	charge	magnetic poles	polarization

WORKING WITH MAGNETS

Directions: Work in teams of two as you perform your first activity. Gather these materials as directed by your teacher.

TEAM MATERIALS

- books
- index cards
- iron filings
- large and small paper clips
- magnets (any type or combination of magnets)—1 for each partner
- needles or pins

- paper plates
- rulers
- scratch paper
- small "finishing" nails
- steel nails

GETTING STARTED

1. Study the magnets shown in the illustrations below. Find the type of magnet you are working with and circle it.

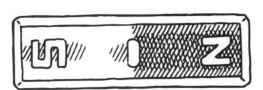

bar magnet

horseshoe magnet

disk magnet

flat, rectangular magnet

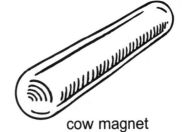

cow magnet

2. Use your magnet to test what it is attracted to. Make a list of some of the materials in the room that you and your partner discover the magnet is attracted to or not attracted to.

You will want to check desks, pens, chairs, window sills, doors, locks, handles, light fixtures, and as many other things as you can. **Note: Do not place magnets on or near computers or other electronic devices.**

List the materials attracted to your magnet and those not attracted to your magnet:

Attracted to: Not attracted to:

_____   _____

_____   _____

_____   _____

_____   _____

WORKING WITH MAGNETS

TESTING MAGNET STRENGTH

Directions: Use several large paper clips, nails, nuts, bolts, screws or similar materials to test how much weight your one magnet will pull and how much it will lift.

Each large paper clip is about two grams in weight. (Some weigh 2.4 grams.)

1. How many large paper clips did your magnet pull? _____

2. How many large paper clips did your magnet lift off the table? _____

   Do the exact same test with your partner's magnet.

3. How many large paper clips did your partner's magnet pull? _____

4. How many large paper clips did your partner's magnet lift off the table? _____

   Combine your two magnets. Let them attach themselves to each other in a row or sitting next to each other.

5. How many large paper clips will they pull together? _____

6. How many large paper clips did the combined magnets lift off the table? _____

TEAMING UP

Join another team and combine the four magnets. Do the same test as before.

1. How many large paper clips did the four magnets pull together? _____

2. How many large paper clips did the four combined magnets lift off the table? _____

3. Decide on another test for your combined "magnet pull and lift."

   Describe your test below and record the results.

   _____

   _____

   _____

NAME _____

WORKING WITH MAGNETS

BECOME A MAGNETIC ARTIST—ETCH YOUR OWN SKETCH

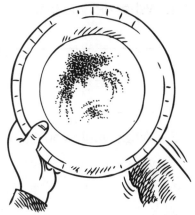

1. Spread a thin layer of iron filings on part of your paper plate. Place your magnet under the plate and move the iron filings around without touching them. Notice that the filings stand up when near the magnet.

2. Create a design or picture with your magnet as if it were a paintbrush moving the paint (iron filings) around on the top of the plate.

3. You may choose to do one design with your partner, or each of you may choose to do your own design. Sketch your design in the box below.

4. Describe what you did in your team. Have you seen an activity like this before? Where?

_____

_____

_____

_____

5. Use a camera, tablet, or cell phone to take a picture of your creation. Share it during the Design Process Review.

WORKING WITH MAGNETS

JOURNAL ENTRY

1. What did you learn about magnets today?

   _____

   _____

   _____

2. What would you like to learn about magnets or their uses?

   _____

   _____

   _____

3. How would a very large magnet be useful around your house or school?

   _____

   _____

   _____

4. How did your design-a-sketch work? What designs or sketches did you make?

   _____

   _____

   _____

5. Which activity did you enjoy the most? Why?

   _____

   _____

   _____

DESIGN PROCESS REVIEW—WORKING WITH MAGNETS

Use your magnet experiences and Journal Entry responses to share questions and ideas with your class in a general class discussion moderated by your teacher.

MAKING MAGNETS BY INDUCTION

Directions: Work in teams of two as you perform this activity. Gather these materials as directed by your teacher.

> **TEAM MATERIALS**
> - iron filings
> - magnets, nails (various sizes—uncoated)
> - paper plates
> - plastic spoons
> - watch or stopwatch

GETTING STARTED
TRIAL 1

1. The results of this experiment will be recorded in the chart on page 105. Rub the magnet down the full length of the nail 10 times. Rub one direction only in a loop, from the head of the nail to the tip, so that the magnet is only near the nail as it actually touches the nail. **Rubbing the magnet back-and-forth will not work.**

2. Hold the nail above the paper plate of iron filings. Approximately how much of the spoonful of iron filings did your magnetized nail attract? Did it attract $\frac{1}{4}$, $\frac{1}{2}$, or more of the spoonful? Did it fail to attract any filings?

   _____

3. How long did it take for the filings to fall off the nail? Did they stay for about 1 minute, 3 minutes, or longer? Did moving the nail cause more filings to drop off?

   _____

4. Wipe any remaining iron filings off the nail. Rub the magnet 20 more times in the same direction you did before. Use the nail to attract the iron filings from the plate again.

   Approximately how much of the spoonful of iron filings did your magnetized nail attract this time? Did it attract $\frac{1}{4}$, $\frac{1}{2}$, or more of the spoonful? Did it fail to attract any filings?

   _____

   Was there any significant difference in the number of filings the nail attracted this time?

   _____

5. Leave the nail and filings undisturbed while you do this next test. Wait two minutes. Are the filings still sticking to the nail? Have some fallen off? Pick up the nail. Do any more filings fall off? What do you think is happening to the temporary nail magnet?

   _____

   _____

MAKING MAGNETS BY INDUCTION

TRIAL 2

1. Use the magnet to pick up any stray iron filings off of the nail. Wipe the filings off the magnet and place them back on the plate.

   Reverse the direction of the nail. Rub the magnet over the nail from the tip to the head. Rub it 10 times. Try to pick up the iron filings from the plate by using the head and top of the nail.

   What fraction of the filings did your nail attract: less than $\frac{1}{4}$, $\frac{1}{4}$, $\frac{1}{2}$, or more? Did it fail to attract any filings?

   _____

2. Wipe any remaining iron filings off the nail. Rub the magnet in the same direction as the previous step 20 times. Use the nail to attract the iron filings from the plate again.

3. Did your nail attract more filings with the extra 10 rubs? Explain in detail what happened.

   _____

   _____

   _____

MAKING MAGNETS BY INDUCTION

Record the results of your experiments in the table below and share your findings with the class. Then type up your procedure on a computer by using the procedure outlined on the next page.

	TRIAL 1 (10)	TRIAL 2 (10)	TRIAL 1 (20)	TRIAL 2 (20)
Team 1				
Team 2				
Team 3				
Team 4				
Team 5				
Team 6				
Team 7				
Team 8				
Team 9				
Team 10				
Team 11				
Team 12				
Team 13				
Team 14				
Team 15				
Team 16				
Team 17				
Team 18				

MAKING MAGNETS BY INDUCTION

Directions: Use a computer to make a table like the one on page 105 to compare the amount of filings picked up by a nail that was rubbed 10 times and one that was rubbed 20 times.

CHARTING RESULTS—TECHNOLOGY PROCEDURES

1. Open **Word** or **Google Docs**.

2. Click on the **Table** and insert a table. You will need to fill in how many rows and columns you need.

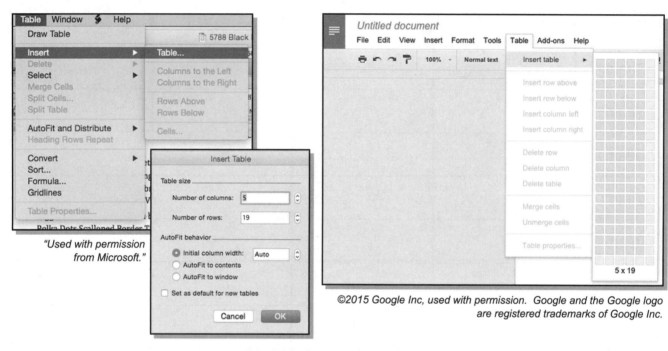

"Used with permission from Microsoft."

©2015 Google Inc, used with permission. Google and the Google logo are registered trademarks of Google Inc.

3. The table should have 5 columns and 19 rows.

4. Your empty table will appear on your page.

5. You can make adjustments by going back to **Table** on the menu bar. You can make the size of the cells different, and you can add or delete rows and columns.

6. Label the table and fill in the teams and approximately how many filings the temporary magnets picked up: $\frac{1}{4}$, $\frac{1}{2}$, $\frac{3}{4}$, ALL.

MAKING MAGNETS BY INDUCTION

JOURNAL ENTRY

1. What did you learn about inducing magnetism (making a temporary magnet) in this activity?

   _____

   _____

   _____

2. Did you notice the nail working better at picking up filings in Trial 1 or Trial 2? Why do you think this was the case?

   _____

   _____

   _____

3. How would you have changed this experiment to find out more information?

   _____

   _____

   _____

4. What other materials in the classroom could have been safely magnetized using this method?

   _____

   _____

   _____

DESIGN PROCESS REVIEW—MAKING MAGNETS BY INDUCTION

Use your Journal Entry, table, and observations in a class discussion led by your teacher.

CREATING ELECTROMAGNETS

Directions: Work with a partner to create an electromagnet using the materials listed below.

TEAM MATERIALS

- aluminum foil
- batteries (C, D, AA, or AAA)
- battery holder or large wide rubber bands
- iron filings
- magnets, nails (various sizes—uncoated)

- paper clips or metal flanges
- paper or plastic plates
- plastic spoons
- small pieces of sandpaper
- thin coated wire

GETTING STARTED

1. Working with a partner, assemble your battery apparatus in any of the following ways:

   a. Place a large D cell battery in a plastic battery holder or rubber band and fit two metal brackets, large paper clips, or metal flanges on each side of the battery in the battery holder.

   or

   b. Place a smaller C cell, AA, or AAA battery in the battery holder, hold it in place with a small wad of aluminum foil, and fit two metal brackets, large paper clips, or metal flanges on each side of the battery in the battery holder.

   or

   c. Tightly wrap a D cell or C cell battery with a wide rubber band— lengthwise around each end—and fit two metal brackets, large paper clips, or metal flanges on each side of the battery, under the rubber band.

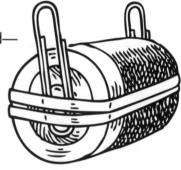

2. Complete the assembly this way:

   a. Wrap a 6- or 8-inch-long coated piece of thin wire around a nail; leave 1 inch of bare wire at each end. (See Unit 1, page 22 for stripping coated wire with sandpaper.)

   b. Attach one bare end of the wire to one paper clip or flange touching the battery.

   c. Attach the other bare end of the wire to the remaining paper clip or flange touching the battery. Sketch your completed electromagnet in the box below.

CREATING ELECTROMAGNETS

USING THE ELECTROMAGNET

1. Test your completed electromagnet by touching one end of the nail (head or point) to a metal object. It should pick it up or pull at it.

2. Spread your iron filings on a paper or plastic plate. Try using the point of the nail in the electromagnet to pick up some of the iron filings.

   Did you get $\frac{1}{4}$, $\frac{1}{2}$, $\frac{3}{4}$, all, or none of the filings?

   _____

   (If no filings were picked up, make sure your electromagnet is hooked up properly.)

3. Spread the filings out on the plate again. Try to pick the filings up, this time using the head of the nail.

   Did you get $\frac{1}{4}$, $\frac{1}{2}$, $\frac{3}{4}$, all, or none of the filings?

   _____

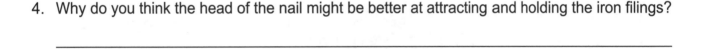

   Which end of the electromagnet worked best—the head of the nail or the point?

   _____

4. Why do you think the head of the nail might be better at attracting and holding the iron filings?

   _____

   _____

   _____

   _____

CREATING ELECTROMAGNETS

TESTING YOUR ELECTROMAGNET

1. What other materials was your electromagnet attracted to? Make a list of some of the materials in the room that you and your partner discover the magnet is attracted to or not attracted to. You will want to check desks, pens, chairs, window sills, doors, locks, handles, light fixtures, and as many other things as you can. **(Remember not to use magnets near computers or other electronic devices.)**

_____   _____   _____

_____   _____   _____

2. List which magnet tests stronger—your natural magnet or your electromagnet—at attracting the following metallic items:

_____ a. iron filings

_____ b. small nails

_____ c. large paper clips

_____ d. other metal objects

3. Get together with another pair of students. List which magnet tests stronger—your electromagnet or the other pair's electromagnet—at attracting the following metallic items:

_____ a. iron filings

_____ b. small nails

_____ c. large paper clips

_____ d. other metal objects

You can increase the strength of your electromagnet using any of the following:

a. Increase the length of wire wrapped around the nail (add more coils around the nail.)

b. Use a stronger, newer, or additional battery.

c. Add another nail to the core of the electromagnet.

d. Use a combination of all three.

You will test these strategies on the next page.

CREATING ELECTROMAGNETS

HOW TO STRENGTHEN AN ELECTROMAGNET

Directions:

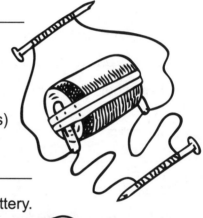

A. Add a 6-inch wire to the one you have, or use a foot-long wire. Make sure the wire ends are stripped and connected as shown in the illustration on the right.

Wrap the wire in coils around the nail as many times as you can, leaving 1 inch of wire on each end.

How many more iron filings did the nail with the extra coils of wire pick up?

_____

B. Add another nail to the electromagnet. The point of the new nail can face up or down with respect to the other nail. Re-wrap the wire around both nails.

How many more iron filings did the extra nail (plus extra coils) pick up?

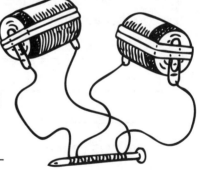

_____

C. Add a second battery, a bigger battery, or a fresh (newer) battery.

How many more iron filings did the new or extra battery (plus extra nail and extra coils) pick up?

_____

D. Pick one other change to make to your electromagnet that will strengthen it. Describe what you added and how it worked.

_____

_____

Sketch and label the design of your strongest electromagnet in the box below.

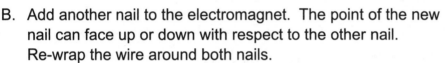

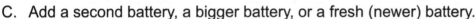

CREATING ELECTROMAGNETS

JOURNAL ENTRY

1. What did you learn today about electromagnets?

_____

_____

_____

2. What do you think electromagnets are used for around the house, at school, in business, or in transportation? What kinds of equipment would they be used in?

_____

_____

_____

3. How could you compare the strength of two electromagnets?

_____

_____

_____

4. Which do you think is stronger—your electromagnet or a natural magnet? How would you test the strength of each magnet?

_____

_____

_____

5. What was your most interesting experiment today? Why?

_____

_____

_____

DESIGN PROCESS REVIEW—CREATING ELECTROMAGNETS

Share your Journal Entry responses and your magnet experiences in the class discussion moderated by your teacher.

MAGNET POWER CHALLENGE

CHALLENGE ACTIVITY—OPTION #1: CREATING EFFECTIVE MAGNETS

Challenge Assignment: Create the most effective magnetic tool by using the materials provided. Use the materials provided (or allowed) to create a magnetic tool to perform one or more activities described. You may use the Design Process Worksheet on page 5 to help you.

1. You may create an electromagnet, a magnet created by induction such as a nail, or a combination of small magnets and magnetic material.

2. Your invention may be used to lift or move a variety of small objects. It may combine small magnets and an electromagnet.

3. Your invention may combine small disk magnets, bar magnets, horseshoe magnets, electromagnets, and metals.

4. Your invention may involve an artistic design done by two partners, a checkerboard game design, or a puzzle layout.

A PLACE TO START—MAKE A CRANE

> ### MATERIALS
> - 1 small, light rectangular or disk magnet
> - fishing line (8 lb. test or stronger is best)
> - flexible metal such as a coat hanger or the fastener for a report holder
> - paper clips or thin rubber bands
> - small metal objects
> - tape
> - thin, flexible metal strips about 1 inch (2.5 cm) wide and about 11.5 inches (30 cm) long (or longer)

1. Place one thin metal strip partly under a thick book to hold it in place. You can use masking tape to hold the metal firmly on your desk instead of the book.

2. Attach a piece of the report holder fastener or another metal piece to make a frame for your model lifter. Slide one piece into another if it will fit. If they don't fit into each other, firmly tape them together. Bend the last part forward into the air, like a crane. It will look somewhat like this:

3. Tape a piece of fishing line about 18 to 24 inches long to the metal piece at the bottom.

4. Feed the fishing line through holes in the metal frame if there are any. Use one or two paper clips to hold the fishing line on the frame if there are no holes. Thin rubber bands will also hold the line on the frame.

MAGNET POWER CHALLENGE

CHALLENGE ACTIVITY—OPTION #1: CREATING EFFECTIVE MAGNETS *(cont.)*

5. Tie or tape a small disk or rectangular magnet to a piece of fishing line and tie the other end to the end of the crane. Make sure the magnet on the line can reach the desk.

6. Use a large paper clip as the crane's lifter. Bend the paper clip to a 90-degree angle as shown below. Tape the fishing line to the paper clip near the bottom of the crane. The paper clip should stay firmly attached to the fishing line.

7. Practice winding up the paper clip lifter. It should wind up the fishing line and slowly pull the magnet (and its load) up the crane to the top.

NAME _____

MAGNET POWER CHALLENGE

CHALLENGE ACTIVITY—OPTION #2: DESIGNING GAMES

Directions: Design your own game that uses magnets and metal objects. The suggestions below are for a simple game. Make yours more complicated, detailed, or entirely different. You may use the Design Process Worksheet on page 5 to help you.

> ### MATERIALS
> - Bristol board, poster board, manila folder, piece of tagboard, or similar material
> - markers
> - paper clips
> - pencil
> - ruler
> - scissors
> - small disk or rectangular magnets
> - tape

1. Make a game board 12 inches by 12 inches or 10 inches square. Use the ruler to carefully measure the tagboard or Bristol board. Cut it to size.

2. Use the ruler to mark the inch marks along one side—on the top and again at the bottom.

3. Check that the dots line up, then draw lines from top to bottom.

4. Measure 1-inch spaces across the third side of the paper and then 1-inch spaces on the remaining side, opposite the side you just did.

5. Make sure these dots line up, then draw connecting lines.

6. You can—but don't have to—draw identical lines on the reverse side. (You should be able to feel the spaces with your fingertips.)

7. If you made a 10-inch board, there should be 10 rows, with 10 spaces in each row, making 100 spaces. If you made a 12-inch board, you should have 12 rows, with 12 spaces in each row, making 144 spaces.

MAGNET POWER CHALLENGE

CHALLENGE ACTIVITY—OPTION #2: DESIGNING GAMES (cont.)

PLAYING THE GAME

You will want to design your own game but first practice with this simple game.

1. Use a marker and tape to mark five small paper clips red. Use another marker and tape to mark five small paper clips black (or some other color).

2. Tape one end of the game board to the edge of one desk, and the other end to the edge of a second desk. The board should be flat across the two desks and open underneath.

3. You and your partner can play this game together. Each partner needs a small magnet to move the paper clips from underneath.

4. You must move the pieces with magnets only.

RULES

1. Each partner uses his or her magnet to manipulate their own colored paper clips from beneath the board.

2. A player can only move one of his or her clips one or two spaces at one time in any **one** direction.

3. In one turn, you may move your paper clips forward, backward, sideways, or diagonally.

4. You cannot land on a space where another player's paper clip or one of your own paper clips is already placed.

5. You cannot go through a space where another player's paper clip is already placed. You must go around it.

6. To win, you must move all five of your paper clips, using the rules above, from the side you started on to the other side—before your partner gets all five of his or her pieces to your side.

MAGNET POWER CHALLENGE

CHALLENGE ACTIVITY—OPTION #2: DESIGNING GAMES *(cont.)*

DESIGN YOUR OWN GAME

Directions: Create a game of your own using magnets and available materials. It may be similar to the one on the previous page or entirely different. You may use the Design Process Worksheet on page 5 to help you.

NOTE: The design must be able to be created using the available materials.

List your ideas here:

1. _____
2. _____
3. _____
4. _____
5. _____
6. _____

Discuss the merits and problems of each idea with your team. Make sure you have the materials needed to create the game. Get teacher approval.

Describe your chosen game, including the rules and how to win.

_____

_____

_____

_____

List the steps in making the game:

1. _____
2. _____
3. _____
4. _____
5. _____
6. _____

Play your finished game.

 NAME _____

MAGNET POWER CHALLENGE

CHALLENGE ACTIVITY—OPTION #3: CREATE YOUR OWN ELECTROMAGNET

Directions: Use the materials available in your class to make an electromagnet for a special purpose, such as the suggestions below:

- See how powerful you can make an electromagnet, using available materials.

- Design a game that uses an electromagnet.

- Use an electromagnet with the crane from the earlier project in order to pick up things.

- Use an electromagnet to check possible magnetic materials.

NOTE: Check your materials and the safety of your project with your teacher before beginning.

You may use the Design Process Worksheet on page 5 to help you.

List materials needed:

_____   _____   _____

_____   _____   _____

_____   _____   _____

Purpose of the electromagnet:

_____

_____

_____

Sketch your electromagnet:

MAGNET POWER CHALLENGE

CHALLENGE ACTIVITY—JOURNAL ENTRY

Use a computer, tablet, or other device to respond to each paragraph subject below. Use complete sentences and describe your experiences clearly.

PARAGRAPH 1

Which challenge project did you do, and why did you choose that project?

PARAGRAPH 2

What did you learn about magnets in this unit that you didn't know before?

PARAGRAPH 3

Which was the most challenging activity in this magnets unit? Why was it difficult?

PARAGRAPH 4

What would you do differently if you could do the magnet unit over again? Why?

PARAGRAPH 5

Respond to these questions by referring back to the activities you completed in this unit.

1. *What are permanent magnets?*

2. *How can you make a magnet out of a nail or other metal object?*

3. *How strong is the temporary magnet?*

4. *How long does the temporary magnet retain its magnetic force?*

5. *What materials will magnets attract or be attracted to?*

DESIGN PROCESS REVIEW—MAGNET POWER CHALLENGE

Share your investigation, experiences, and Journal Entry responses with your classmates in the class discussion your teacher leads to culminate this unit.

WORKING WITH MOTORS

4 Sessions: 1 session per each activity (approximately 1 to $1\frac{1}{2}$ hours per session)

CONNECTIONS AND SUGGESTIONS

SCIENCE—The motor activities in this book are done with a 1.5-volt motor powered by a C or D cell battery. Many of the activities involve circular motion/centripetal motion as the motor rotates the cards, creating illusions. The circular motion of the motor keeps the marble holder in motion and causes the marble to move up the tube, where it is clearly visible to students. All of these activities reflect the effects of circular motion. This is true of the color wheel in motion, as well as the other art effects.

TECHNOLOGY—The motor provides a technological application to the color wheel and the other illusions by putting them in motion. The motorized-marbles activity is another application of technology. Students use computer technology to keep records and to report on their projects.

ENGINEERING—Students will experiment with several engineering designs for the motors and associated equipment to produce functioning apparatuses to create illusions and motorize marbles.

MATH—Students will use compasses and protractors to produce and measure angles.

Materials

- C or D cell batteries
- clear tape
- colored markers
- film canisters
- ice cubes
- index cards
- large rubber bands
- manila folders
- marbles
- math compasses
- sturdy paper or plastic cups
- paper clips
- paper/plastic bowls or plates
- pieces of white paper

- protractors
- push pins
- roll of clear transparent plastic
- roll of masking tape
- rulers
- scissors
- small electric or DC motors
- small film canisters (see note below)
- small squares of sandpaper (about 2 inches square)
- straws
- thin wire (22 gauge or less—preferably coated wire)

NOTE: Most of these materials are reusable. The motors usually last for years. The film canisters can be purchased from plastic retailers on the Internet for about 25 to 40 cents each. Photo supply stores sell them in bulk.

UNIT 6 VOCABULARY

<u>arc</u>—a part of the circumference of a circle or other curve

<u>canister</u>—a small plastic (or metal) container

<u>compass</u>—a math tool for making circles and arcs

<u>gravity</u>—the force that pulls objects toward the center of Earth

<u>illusions</u>—images or pictures that appear different from how they really are

<u>intersecting lines</u>—lines that cross each other

<u>lead wires</u>—short connecting wires extending from a motor

<u>negative terminal (−)</u>—one of two electrical contacts of a dry-cell battery (for round batteries, the negative terminal is the flat end)

<u>positive terminal (+)</u>—one of two electrical contacts of a dry-cell battery (for round batteries, the positive terminal is the raised end)

<u>protractor</u>—a tool for measuring angles

<u>transparency</u>—a thin, clear sheet of plastic

DISCUSSION PROMPT:

These days we see motors used for everything from cars to office equipment to robots. Motors have definitely helped shape how we live our lives and make many aspects of our lives easier. Riding in a car to get somewhere faster than walking and using a microwave oven to heat food quickly are just two examples of using motors in our daily lives. What are some ways that you use motors in your everyday life? What is your favorite motorized machine or object to use, and why?

MOTORS

A motor is a machine that is designed to convert one form of energy into mechanical energy. The first electric motor was built in 1928 by Anyos Jedlik, a Hungarian inventor. He was also an engineer, physicist, Benedictine priest, and author. He started experimenting with electromagnetic rotating devices that he called "lighting-magnetic self-rotors." These contained three main components: the stator (the stationary part of a rotary system), the rotor (the piece that directs the magnetic field of a magnet), and the commutator (the moving cylinder on the rotating portion of a motor). The original motor is kept at the Museum of Applied Arts in Budapest and is said to still work perfectly today!

first electric motor

A common motor that many of us use daily is a motor vehicle or automobile, like a car or truck. It is self-propelled and does not need rails like trains or trolleys. Some vehicles use electric motors that convert electrical energy into mechanical energy. Others use what is called an internal combustion engine, which converts thermal energy to mechanical energy. This is done using heat, air, and fuel (like gasoline) to cause a chemical reaction. Karl Benz is credited with being the inventor of the first automobile powered by an internal combustion engine, called the "Motorwagen." It was the first motorized vehicle that completely generated its own power, unlike the motorized-stage coach that also used horses. It was also the first commercially available automobile in history.

early combustion-engine automobile

While vehicles use their motors to convert electrical or thermal energy into mechanical energy, other machines use kinetic energy to generate mechanical energy and electricity. Wind turbines are connected to generators that use rotors to create electromagnetic induction (voltage), which generates electricity. The generators are able to rotate the rotors by the movement of the wind turbine blades. As the wind passes the turbines, it moves the blades, which in turn spins the shaft of the generator. The wind can also be used as mechanical power for things such as pumping water or grinding grain.

wind turbines

Use a computer or tablet to search for information on the Internet to help you as you complete the activities in this unit. Helpful search terms include:

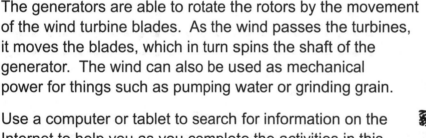

| centripetal motion | force | machine |
| circular motion | illusions | motor |

GETTING ACQUAINTED WITH MOTORS

Directions: Work in teams of two as you perform your first activity. Gather these materials as directed by your teacher.

TEAM MATERIALS

- 2 short pieces (about 3 inches long) of thin wire (preferably coated wire with both ends on both wires stripped about $\frac{3}{4}$ of an inch)
- C or D cell batteries
- ice cubes
- index cards (3 × 5 and 4 × 6)
- manila folders
- math compasses
- paper clips
- paper/plastic bowls or plates
- pieces of white paper
- protractors
- push pins or straight pins
- roll of masking tape
- rulers
- scissors
- small electric (DC) motors
- small squares of sandpaper (about 2 inches square)
- wide rubber bands

GETTING STARTED

(**NOTE:** For the 3 × 5 index cards, only one cut/line will need to be made.)

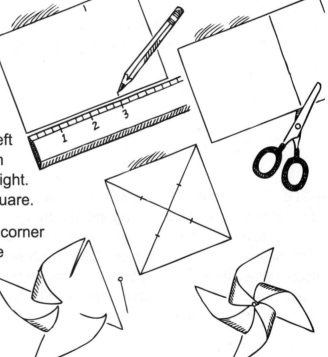

1. Use a ruler to measure a 3-inch square on an index card. Place the ruler at one corner of the card. Measure the long way and draw a small line at the 3-inch point. Then measure three inches down on the card from the 3-inch mark you made going across and mark the spot.

2. Measure three inches down from the top left corner and make a mark. Draw a line from this spot to the "x" you made at the lower right. This should form a square. Cut out the square.

3. Draw a straight diagonal line from the first corner to the opposite corner. Draw a second line connecting the two remaining corners.

4. Make 1-inch cuts along the lines from each of the four corners. Fold the left corner of each triangle to the right at a 90-degree angle.

5. Use a pushpin to make a tiny hole in the center of the card for mounting the card on the motor. This card will be the "fan."

GETTING ACQUAINTED WITH MOTORS

ASSEMBLING THE FAN

1. Place the fan you just made on the central pole of the motor. You may need to use a little masking tape to attach it to the shaft if it is loose or if the hole is too large.

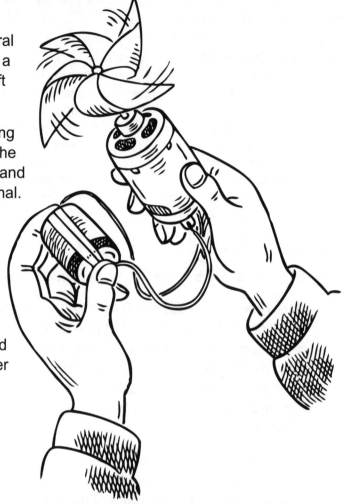

2. If your motor has two wire leads extending from the body, just connect one lead to the positive terminal of a C or D cell battery and the other wire lead to the negative terminal. The fan will move rapidly as the motor starts. Wrap a wide rubber band tightly around the terminals of the battery and place the bare wire leads under the rubber band to keep them firmly connected to the power source.

   You can also wrap each wire lead around a metal paper clip and then slip the paper clip under the rubber band.

NOTE: If your motor does not have the two wire leads, cut two pieces of thin coated wire each about three inches long. Using the sandpaper, strip the rubber, plastic coating, or cover from the last inch of each end of each wire (see page 22). Insert one end of each wire into the two small holes on top of the motor. Twist each wire until it is firmly in place on each side of the motor. Wrap the other end of each wire around a small or large paper clip, then insert each paper clip between the rubber band and the terminals of the battery. You may want to cover the wires attached to the motor with a strip of masking tape to keep them in place.

NAME _____

GETTING ACQUAINTED WITH MOTORS

ASSEMBLING THE FAN *(cont.)*

3. Once you have connected the battery to your motor and fan, the fan will turn rapidly. You and your partner should test your fan and then create some of the designs described below.

LARGER FAN

A. Measure and cut a 4-inch by 4-inch square out of a 4-by-6-inch index card. Draw intersecting diagonal lines from the four corners as you did before. Cut $1\frac{1}{2}$ inches along each line. Fold each of the four pieces up as you did before (to a 90-degree angle) and use a pin to make a tiny hole in the center. Then attach it to the motor.

Does it provide more wind? _____

Does it move just as fast as the first model?

_____

CIRCULAR FAN

A. Use a compass to draw a circle on a 3-by-5-inch or 4-by-6-inch index card. Draw a dot in the center of the circle where the point of your compass was placed. Cut the circle out. Use a ruler to draw a line through the center of the circle from one side to the other. Place a protractor along the line at the exact center and mark points at 60 degrees, 120 degrees, and 180 degrees on that side of the circle. Turn the protractor around to the other half of the circle and again measure and mark points at 60 degrees and 120 degrees.

B. Draw two more straight lines from the points you made through the center of the circle to the points below. The circle should now have six equal spaces.

C. Cut one inch along each line from the outer edge. Fold each cut to the right at a 90-degree angle. Use a pin to make a tiny hole in the center. Place this circular fan on the shaft of the motor, and use a small bit of masking tape to hold it in place.

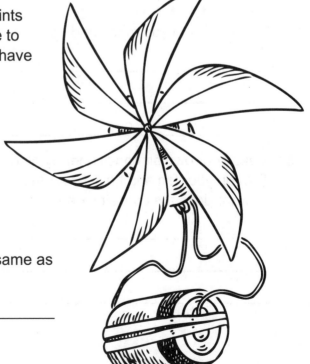

Does this fan work better, worse, or the same as the first design?

_____

 _____

GETTING ACQUAINTED WITH MOTORS

ASSEMBLING THE FAN *(cont.)*

YOUR OWN DESIGN

4. Use your own choice of materials—cards, manila folders, paper—to create your own fan design. Sketch your setup in the box below.

Describe what you made and how it worked. Share your design with the class.

_____

_____

_____

5. Make your own air conditioner by placing three or four ice cubes in a bowl or paper plate. Turn on your fan and hold it over the ice, blowing toward you. Can you feel the cool air? How far does the cool air extend?

_____

_____

_____

 _____

GETTING ACQUAINTED WITH MOTORS

JOURNAL ENTRY

1. Which fan design worked best for you? Why was it the best?

   _____

   _____

   _____

2. Which design in your class did you like best? Why?

   _____

   _____

   _____

3. Why do you think paper would be harder to work with than index cards or manila folders?

   _____

   _____

   _____

4. What other things could you design and use with your motor?

   _____

   _____

   _____

5. Would a very large fan—six inches in diameter or more—work with the motor? How would you make it?

   _____

   _____

   _____

6. What other circular designs could you make for your motor?

   _____

   _____

   _____

DESIGN PROCESS REVIEW—GETTING ACQUAINTED WITH MOTORS

Describe your experiences, difficulties, successes, and challenges with the class during a discussion moderated by your teacher.

NAME _____

MOTORIZED ILLUSIONS

Directions: Work in teams of two as you perform this activity. Gather these materials as directed by your teacher.

TEAM MATERIALS

- 3 × 5 or 4 × 6 inch index cards
- at least 1 motor for each team
- C or D cell batteries
- clear tape
- colored markers—thin and wide
- masking tape
- math compass
- protractor
- push pins
- rulers
- scissors
- sturdy paper or plastic cups for each team

MAKING A COLOR WHEEL

1. Use a math compass to create a full circle on a 3 × 5 or 4 × 6 inch index card. Draw a dot in the center of the circle where the point of your compass was placed.

2. Carefully cut out the circle. Draw a straight line through the dot at the center of your circle. Place your protractor on the line, with the center of the protractor lined up with the center dot.

3. Place marks on the edge of the circle at 60 degrees, 120 degrees, and 180 degrees (should be the edge of your line). Turn the protractor and mark the other side of the circle the same way. You will have six equal marks, 60 degrees apart.

4. Use a ruler to draw a straight line connecting each set of opposite marks.

5. Color each of the six sections of the color wheel with a different color of the spectrum: red, orange, yellow, green, blue, and violet.

6. Use a push pin to make a small hole in the center of the color wheel. Mount the color wheel on the motor shaft. Use a very small bit of clear tape to hold the wheel in place on the shaft.

7. Connect the motor and battery as you've done in previous activities, attaching one wire lead from the motor to each terminal of the battery. Observe the wheel in motion, then disconnect the battery before starting the next step.

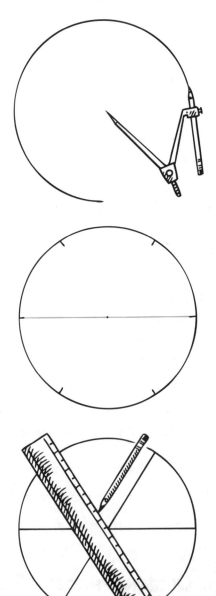

MOTORIZED ILLUSIONS

MAKING A DISPLAY SITE FOR YOUR MOTORIZED ART

1. Turn one 8-ounce or larger paper or plastic cup upside down on your desk. Use masking tape to attach it to the desk, near an edge where it will not interfere with your use of the desk. Tape another large cup right next to the first cup.

2. Place the motor and color wheel on the first cup and use a long piece of masking tape to tape the motor with the color wheel flat on the first cup. Make sure the color wheel rotates freely.

3. Tape the battery on the cup next to the motor.

4. Make sure you have wrapped a wide rubber band around the battery to firmly hold the wire leads from the motor.

5. Attach the bare ends of each wire lead to a large paper clip. Place one of the large paper clips between a battery terminal and the rubber band.

6. Touch the remaining paper clip to the other terminal of the battery. Observe the results and record them on the next page. You can put this remaining paper clip under the rubber band on this terminal if you want the wheel to whirl for an extended period of time.

 NAME _____

MOTORIZED ILLUSIONS

OBSERVING THE COLOR WHEEL IN MOTION

The human eye cannot distinguish the separate colors when the disk is moving as rapidly as it does in this activity. The sections of color appear to blur, and it can be hard to distinguish each color.

1. Describe the effect that occurs when your wheel is in motion.

   _____

   _____

2. Which colors seem to be most noticeable?

   _____

3. Which color is barely seen?

   _____

4. Touch the paper clip holding one wire lead to the battery. Then remove the clip. How do the colors change as the wheel slows down?

   _____

   _____

5. Touch the paper clip holding one wire lead to the battery, pull it back, and touch it again. Do this several times. Describe the results below.

   _____

   _____

   _____

6. Reconnect your color wheel and observe it for 3 or 4 minutes. Describe what changes seem to occur as it rotates. In the box to the right, sketch your color wheel in motion.

   _____

   _____

   _____

   _____

   _____

MOTORIZED ILLUSIONS

CREATING YOUR OWN ILLUSIONS

Directions: For the following activities, use two index cards and cut one to the dimensions of 3 inches by 3 inches and the other cut to 4 inches by 4 inches. You may also use a math compass to make two circles, or you may want to make two triangles.

1. Create a line design on the 3-inch card by using bold slashes of various colors with a wide-tipped marker. Make all the lines horizontal (going side-to-side) with alternating light and dark colors. On the reverse side of the card, create a vertical design (going up-and-down) using the same bold slashes of color.

2. Place your card on the motor—with the horizontal strips of color facing out—and attach it with a thin strip of tape. Start the motor and observe the results.

   Describe the effect:

   _____

   _____

   _____

3. Place your card on the motor—with the vertical lines of color facing out—and attach it with a thin strip of tape. Start the motor and observe the results.

   Describe the effect:

   _____

   _____

   _____

4. Stop your motor. Create a different design on your 4-inch by 4-inch index card. Make two tiny balls of masking tape, each about the size of a pea. Make sure some of the sticky part of the tape is on the outside of each ball. Carefully stick the two small tape balls between the 3-inch and the 4-inch cards so there is some distance between the cards. Attach your cards with the 3-inch card facing out, and connect your motor. Observe the results of this design with the separation. Describe what you see.

   _____

   _____

   _____

MOTORIZED ILLUSIONS

CREATING YOUR OWN ILLUSIONS *(cont.)*

5. Draw a cartoon picture of a "mad scientist" with a face and a lab coat on a new index card. Tape this cartoon on the shaft of your motor. Touch the disconnected paper clip and wire to the end of the battery. Describe what the cartoon looks like when it is motorized.

_____

_____

6. Draw a picture of a book cover on an index card with the title in large letters and a picture of a character, a house, and/or a field. Use thin line markers or dark colored pencils. Tape this book cover illustration on the shaft of your motor. Touch the disconnected paper clip and wire to the end of the battery. Describe what the book cover looks like when it is motorized.

_____

_____

7. Create your own illusions. Motorize them, then sketch and describe the results below.

_____

_____

MOTORIZED ILLUSIONS

JOURNAL ENTRY

1. Which of the designs you made was the most surprising to you? What did you not expect?

   _____

   _____

   _____

2. What did you not expect about the color wheel design?

   _____

   _____

   _____

3. What could you have added to the two index card designs to get a different effect? How would you do it?

   _____

   _____

   _____

4. What two shapes or designs could you combine to get an entirely different effect? How would you combine them or layer them on the motor?

   _____

   _____

   _____

5. What happens to the motor and the speed of the cards when several are hooked onto the shaft?

   _____

   _____

   _____

DESIGN PROCESS REVIEW—MOTORIZED ILLUSIONS

Share your Journal Entry responses and experiences with your classmates in a discussion led by your teacher.

MOTORIZED MARBLES

Directions: Work in teams of two as you perform this activity. Gather these materials as directed by your teacher.

> ## TEAM MATERIALS
> - at least 1 motor for each team of 2 students
> - C or D cell batteries
> - clear tape
> - marbles (various sizes)
> - masking tape
> - plastic or paper cups
> - pushpins
> - roll of clear plastic material (such as projector roll transparency film)
> - round plastic film canisters
> - scissors

ASSEMBLY

1. Collect a sturdy plastic film canister. Use a pushpin to make a hole in the center of the bottom of the canister. Wiggle the pushpin slightly to make the hole a little bigger.

2. Try to insert the shaft of the motor into the hole. You want it to fit, but not be loose.

   You may need to use the pushpin again to make the hole just large enough to insert the shaft from the motor.

3. Connect the motor to the battery as you've done in previous activities. The canister should spin on the motor firmly without coming off. Disconnect the motor and remove the cannister for the next step.

4. Cut a strip of clear, stiff transparency material about 4 inches wide and 12 inches long. Roll it into a long, thin tube and insert it into the plastic film canister. Use a strip of clear, transparent tape to attach it to the canister and a long strip of clear tape to make the plastic into a long tube in the canister. Use a piece of clear tape to make sure the top of the tube is connected.

5. Place the shaft of the motor into the film canister. It should sit firmly and not wobble. (If it does wobble, place a little masking tape over the hole in the canister and then insert the motor shaft again.)

6. Attach the motor to the C or D cell battery to see how it works. The canister with the clear transparent tube should rotate as you hold the motor. The battery can sit on the upside-down cup as it did in the previous activity.

   In the box to the right, sketch your setup.

MOTORIZED MARBLES

MARBLES IN MOTION

Once your motor apparatus is assembled, unhook one side of the battery by removing the paper clip from one terminal of the battery. Leave the clip attached to the motor wire lead.

Place one marble in the plastic tube. It will sit in the bottom of the canister on the shaft of the motor.

Reattach the large paper clip with the other wire lead to the unconnected terminal of the battery.

Hold your motorized marble upright for a minute or two to get used to the motion and movement of the marble. Gradually tip the motor and marble tube on its side so that it is horizontal to the ground.

⚠ **CAUTION!** **Never look directly into the marble tube while the motor is moving.**

Describe what happened.

_____

_____

Slowly tip the motor and marble holder so that it is tipping toward the floor at an angle of about 45 degrees. What is happening to the marble? Did it roll out onto the floor, or is it still in the tube? Is the marble in the same place or closer to the end of the tube?

_____

_____

_____

1. Gradually point the marble holder down until it is vertical with the floor. Make sure the motor is still rotating at the same speed. At what angle with the floor did the marble fall?

   _____

2. Try a smaller, lighter marble in your Motorized Marble Machine. Point it in each direction as you did with the previous marble. Does the power of the motor overcome the weight of the marble? Describe your experiences.

   _____

   _____

   _____

MULTIPLE MOVING MARBLES

Turn your tube so that it is facing up. One member of the team needs to keep the equipment working while the other member of the team tries putting two small, light marbles into the tube. Does the motor manage to keep both marbles in motion? Are they being lifted up a little or a lot? Is one marble in motion and one still? Will they work when the tube is on its side?

_____

_____

MOTORIZED MARBLES

JOURNAL ENTRY

1. What was the most interesting effect you observed with the motorized marbles? Why?

   _____

   _____

   _____

   _____

   _____

2. When the tube pointed down, was the force of gravity greater than the force created by the motor?

   _____

   _____

   _____

   _____

   _____

3. What did the marbles in the tube look like when the motor was running?

   _____

   _____

   _____

   _____

   _____

DESIGN PROCESS REVIEW—MOTORIZED MARBLES

Discuss your Journal Entry responses and describe your team experiences during the class discussion moderated by your teacher.

MOTORIZED MACHINE INVENTIONS

Challenge Assignment: Using your knowledge from the previous investigations, create your own motorized machine. You may choose to assemble the machines according to any of the suggested activities listed, or create your own. Make sure you use the Design Process Worksheet on page 5 to record your investigation.

CHALLENGE ACTIVITY—SUGGESTED ACTIVITY #1: ART IN MOTION

1. Arrange your motor on one upside-down-paper or plastic cup. Place the battery on another upside-down cup. Hook it up and make sure the motor runs smoothly.

2. Cut an index card about 3- or 4-inches square. Use a pushpin to make a hole in the card to fit on the shaft of the motor. Use masking tape on the shaft of the motor to hold the card in place if necessary.

3. Start the motor and get the card moving.

4. Use a thin marker to draw lines or shapes on the moving card.

5. What is happening to the design?

6. Continue this activity using your own ideas.

CHALLENGE ACTIVITY—SUGGESTED IDEA #2: MAKE YOUR OWN POWER DRILL

1. Arrange your motor on one upside-down-paper or plastic cup. Place the battery on another upside-down cup. Hook it up and make sure the motor runs smoothly.

2. Find a thin straw about 6 inches long (or cut one to that size). Slit one end so that the straw can be taped onto the shaft of the motor—making it about a 6-inch tool.

3. Slit the bottom end of the straw about an inch in two to four places and bend back the slits.

4. Use the "power drill" to move sand or dirt in making a mini garden, mixing dirt and water into a stiff mud, or a variety of other earth-moving or sand-moving projects.

   Continue this activity on your own.

MOTORIZED MACHINE INVENTIONS

CHALLENGE ACTIVITY—SUGGESTED IDEA #3: MAKE A POLISHER

1. Arrange your motor on one upside-down cup. Place the battery on another upside-down cup. Hook it up and make sure the motor runs smoothly.

2. Wrap a 1-inch square piece of rough sandpaper around the shaft of the motor. The sandpaper will extend past the end of the shaft. Use masking tape to keep it in place on the shaft.

3. Use the polisher to polish a nail or sand a stone.

   Continue this activity on your own, using the Design Process Worksheet on page 5 to guide you.

CHALLENGE ACTIVITY—CREATE YOUR OWN PROJECT

Invent your own motorized machine using available materials. List some of your project ideas below. Then, use the Design Process Worksheet on page 5 to record your investigation.

_____

_____

_____

_____

_____

_____

Sketch the model of your motorized machine in the box below.

MOTORIZED MACHINE INVENTIONS

CHALLENGE ACTIVITY—JOURNAL ENTRY

Use a computer, tablet, or other device to write paragraphs for each topic. Use complete sentences and describe your experiences clearly.

PARAGRAPH 1

What was your basic idea for an invention using the motor? Did your idea work? How well?

PARAGRAPH 2

What problems did you encounter in creating your invention? How did you solve these problems?

PARAGRAPH 3

How did you demonstrate your invention? What were the most important things you mentioned about your invention? What didn't you mention?

PARAGRAPH 4

Which was the best invention shown by any team? What made it different from the other inventions? Why was it the best?

PARAGRAPH 5

What would you do next time to improve the product or invention you and your partner created? What one thing might have made it much better? What else would have helped?

PARAGRAPH 6

Respond to these questions by referring back to the activities you completed in this unit.

1. *How can you make illusions with motors?*

2. *How can you make a marble lifter?*

3. *What kind of work can you do with a motor?*

4. *What does a motor need to function?*

5. *What activities can you do with motors?*

DESIGN PROCESS REVIEW—MOTORIZED MACHINE INVENTIONS

Share your investigation, Journal Entry responses, and project observations in your concluding class discussion for this unit.

 **UNIT 7**

BUILDING BRIDGES

> **4 Sessions:** 1 session per each activity (approximately $1\frac{1}{2}$ hours per session)

CONNECTIONS AND SUGGESTIONS

SCIENCE—Students will explore the forces of compression, tension, and load weight by designing bridges to handle these forces in different ways.

TECHNOLOGY—Students will create features of different bridge designs. They will use technology to record results of investigations and tests.

The bridge models form much of the technology in this unit. Students will use technology to create charts for comparing bridge loads and for reporting on their projects, writing their journals, and recording their observations.

ENGINEERING—Students will work with elements of design to produce stronger, more effective bridges. They will integrate design elements of different styles of bridges.

Students will experiment with several engineering designs for the bridges, abutments, frames, arches, and associated equipment in order to produce functioning, effective models of real bridges.

MATH—Students will utilize angle measurements and applications of triangles in building bridges. Comparisons of weight and linear measurement will be taken as well. Students will apply precise metric measurement in building the bridges.

Materials

- 12 rolls of pennies
- drinking straws
- fishing line (10-pound test or stronger)
- index cards
- masking tape
- modeling clay (or moist soil if necessary)
- rulers
- scissors
- sewing pins
- thin stirring straws
- wooden barbeque skewers

NOTE: Most of these materials, especially the clay, are reusable.

UNIT 7 VOCABULARY

<u>abutment</u>—part of the support for a bridge, at its ends

<u>arch bridge</u>—type of bridge in which the arch helps distribute the weight to the abutments at each end of the bridge

<u>beam bridge</u>—simplest type of flat bridge

<u>deck</u>—the surface of a bridge that is used for a roadway or walkway

<u>distribution</u>—the position or arrangement of something throughout a particular space or area, the way it is divided or spread out

<u>suspension bridge</u>—type of long bridge in which cables help support the bridge and distribute some weight to the support towers

<u>truss bridge</u>—bridge type that uses beams forming triangles to distribute and support the load

DISCUSSION PROMPT:

There are many different types of bridges all over the world. There is one type called a *clapper bridge*, formed by large flat slabs of stone, a *pontoon bridge*, which actually floats on the water, and even one called a *pigtail bridge*, which loops over its own road. Why do you think there are so many different kinds of bridges? What are some conditions that would determine what type of bridge you would need for a certain area?

BRIDGES

The bridge activities in this book are designed to create models that replicate the basic features of four types of bridges. The *beam bridge* is the simplest and oldest type of bridge—first used to cross a stream and small rivers. A beam bridge can be as simple as a board thrown across a narrow creek. It is usually flat, made from concrete and metal, extending from one side of a body of water or valley to the other.

beam bridge

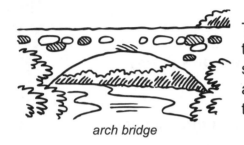

arch bridge

The *arch bridge* is a very old style of bridge but is still used today in many parts of the world. The arch extends to each side of the bridge, distributing some of the load, and therefore allowing heavier loads. Much of the weight is transferred to the abutments on each end of an arch bridge.

The *truss bridge* takes advantage of the strength of the beams when they are arranged in triangles, which form much of the support. This type of bridge distributes the load over a wider area of the bridge, transferring weight to the piers or upright supports of the bridge.

truss bridge

suspension bridge

A *suspension bridge* uses ropes or cables to distribute the load to the towers supporting the base of the bridge. It can be as simple as an ancient rope bridge or a modern suspension bridge such as the Golden Gate Bridge.

Use a computer or tablet to search for information on the Internet to help you as you complete the activities in this unit. Helpful search terms include:

arch bridge	beam bridge	suspension bridge	truss bridge
Sydney Harbor Bridge	Bolsoy Bridge	Brooklyn Bridge	Mississippi River Bridge
		Golden Gate Bridge	

CONSTRUCTING A BEAM BRIDGE

Directions: Work in teams of two as you perform this first activity. Gather these materials as directed by your teacher.

> ### TEAM MATERIALS
> - 8 rolls of pennies
> - 30 cm (1 foot) of masking tape
> - 50 sewing pins
> - 60 thin stirring straws
> - Bristol board, poster board, or index cards
> - rulers
> - scissors

GETTING STARTED

A beam bridge is the simplest form of bridge. You often see one over a small stream on a country road. A beam bridge usually has a flat surface made of wood or asphalt. It was the first kind of bridge to be developed by humans.

ACTIVITY RULES

(These rules apply for each bridge in the unit.)

1. Your bridge must span a length of at least $1\frac{1}{2}$ feet (45 centimeters) between desks. (It will have to be longer than that to firmly connect to each desk.)

2. The beam bridge must be at least 6 inches (15 centimeters) wide at all points.

3. Connect the straws with sewing pins or very thin strips of masking tape. You must be very sparing in the use of the tape or pins. You only get one strip of tape 1 foot (30 centimeters) long and 50 pins to use.

4. You may make any design for the base of this beam bridge, but you only get 60 thin straws to build the bridge.

BUILDING THE BRIDGE

1. The base—or floor—of your bridge needs to be strong and flexible. Make a section of the bridge flooring with interlocking straws placed about 1 to 2 inches apart across both the width and length of this section. You can start this section with four straws for the perimeter, pinned or taped together. Then attach 6 straws an inch apart along the length of this section. Pin or tape the straws across the square. (The pins provide a sturdier frame. Use caution when using the pins.)

2. Make three sections as described above. Attach the sections to each other with three pins at the top, middle, and bottom of the straws.

CONSTRUCTING A BEAM BRIDGE

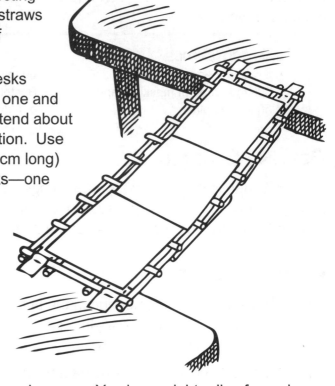

3. Reinforce the bridge with two straws connecting sections along each side and two or three straws connecting sections along the underside of the bridge.

4. Lay your completed bridge between two desks separated by 45 centimeters (the length of one and a half rulers). Your beam bridge should extend about 6 centimeters onto the desks in each direction. Use four small strips of tape (3 mm wide and 3 cm long) to secure the completed bridge to the desks—one strip on each of the four corners.

5. Cover the bridge deck with three index cards, pieces of poster board, or Bristol board cut to the size of the base—about 18 cm (7 inches) square. Use two 3 mm by 3 mm pieces of tape to attach each card to the bridge.

TESTING YOUR BRIDGE

The bridges will be tested individually as the class observes. You have eight rolls of pennies to use as testing weights. You will want to test them starting with one roll and adding a roll for each test. Each penny weighs about 2.5 grams. A roll, therefore, weighs about 125 grams.

1. Place one roll on your bridge. Did the bridge hold? _____

2. Did it bend the bridge? _____

3. Keep adding rolls of pennies. Arrange the rolls so that the weight is spread out over the length of the bridge.

4. Use the chart on the next page to record what happens after each roll of pennies is added to the bridge.

5. Test each bridge in the class, and record the results.

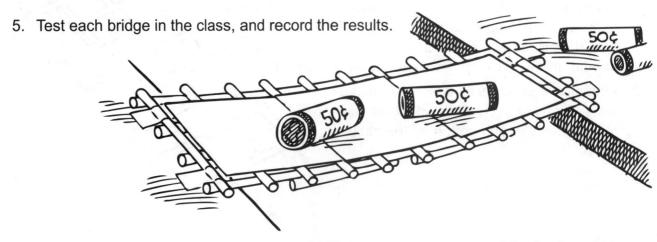

CONSTRUCTING A BEAM BRIDGE

Directions: Use a computer to make a table like the one below.

CHARTING RESULTS—TECHNOLOGY PROCEDURES

1. Open **Word** or **Google Docs**.
2. Click on the **Table** and insert a table. You will need to fill in how many rows and columns you need.

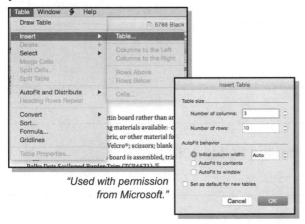

"Used with permission from Microsoft."

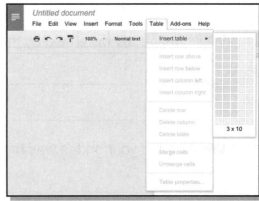

©2015 Google Inc, used with permission. Google and the Google logo are registered trademarks of Google Inc.

3. The table should have 3 columns and 10 rows.
4. Your empty table will appear on your page.
5. You can make adjustments by going back to **Table** on the menu bar. You can make the size of the cells different, and you can add or delete rows and columns.
6. Label the table and fill it in with the results of testing your bridge. Add any notes and observations that you made while you were testing.

BEAM BRIDGE		
WEIGHT USED (PENNIES)	RESULTS	NOTES
1 roll (125 grams)		
2 rolls (250 grams)		
3 rolls (375 grams)		
4 rolls (500 grams)		
5 rolls (625 grams)		
6 rolls (750 grams)		
7 rolls (875 grams)		
8 rolls (1,000 grams)		

CONSTRUCTING A BEAM BRIDGE

OTHER LOADS

Make any necessary repairs to your bridge from the previous activity. Then try using some of the following materials to test your bridge. Many are in your desk or the classroom. Begin testing with the lightest of the materials first.

- box of crayons and/or markers
- notebook
- paperback books
- pencils
- small library books
- stapler

1. Which materials were held by the bridge?

_____

_____

2. What part of your bridge was the weakest and the first to collapse?

_____

_____

3. What could you have improved in your bridge design or construction?

_____

_____

_____

4. Illustrate your bridge below. In your illustration, include one of the loads you used to test the strength of your bridge.

★ ★ ★ SAVE YOUR BEAM BRIDGE FOR THE NEXT ACTIVITY. ★ ★ ★

CONSTRUCTING A BEAM BRIDGE

JOURNAL ENTRY

1. What did you like best about this activity? Why?

_____

_____

_____

2. What problems did you encounter in building this beam bridge?

_____

_____

_____

3. What did you learn about building bridges in this activity?

_____

_____

_____

4. Why did the most successful bridge in the classroom succeed? What did that bridge have that made it successful?

_____

_____

_____

5. If you were doing this activity again, what would you change or improve about your design?

_____

_____

_____

DESIGN PROCESS REVIEW—CONSTRUCTING A BEAM BRIDGE

Share your Journal Entry responses, experiences, and suggestions with the class during the discussion led by your teacher.

CONSTRUCTING AN ARCH BRIDGE

(This activity builds on the previous lesson and incorporates the design features of an arch bridge. You will want to use and repair your beam bridge before adding the arch.)

MATERIALS
- 10 rolls of pennies
- 15 cm of masking tape
- beam bridge (from previous activity)
- modeling clay (preferred) or thick, moist soil (if necessary)
- scissors
- sewing pins
- thin straws

GETTING STARTED

- Repair your beam bridge carefully. Make sure your pins are holding the straws firmly in place. Reapply the small pieces of tape you used to connect the bridge sections. Repair or replace broken or badly damaged straws.

- Creating the arch under the surface of the bridge on your model requires some care. (In real life, the arch would be constructed before the top.) You may use modeling clay and straws for an effective arch. (If modeling clay is not available, use thick, moist soil.)

BUILDING THE ARCH

1. Slit 1 inch of each end of five thin straws.

2. Slip each slit end into the end of another thin straw so that each pair of straws stick together to form one longer straw. These long straws will serve as reinforcements for the clay arch.

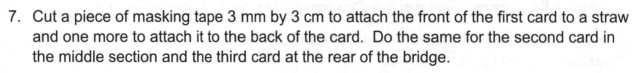

3. Press these five double-length straws through the underside of the beam bridge, in the center of the bridge about 3 cm apart. Arrange the straws so that they stick out about 15 cm in each direction. Arrange the straws so that one straw is about two cm from the edge on one side and the other is about 2 cm from the end of the bridge on the other side. The other three straws can be about 3 cm apart from each other and the end straws.

4. Mold the modeling clay so that it forms curved abutments at each end of your bridge. The clay would go down about 5 cm (2 inches) at the far end of each side of the bridge and gradually arch up to the deck of the bridge about 8 cm (3 inches) toward the middle of the bridge from each end. They will look like the illustration above.

5. Mold the ends of the five straws firmly into the clay on each side of the bridge.

6. Cover the flat deck of the bridge as you did in the first activity with three index cards, pieces of poster board, or pieces of Bristol board cut to fit each section.

7. Cut a piece of masking tape 3 mm by 3 cm to attach the front of the first card to a straw and one more to attach it to the back of the card. Do the same for the second card in the middle section and the third card at the rear of the bridge.

CONSTRUCTING AN ARCH BRIDGE

TESTING THE ARCH BRIDGE

The bridges can be tested individually as the class observes. You have 10 rolls of pennies to use as testing weights. Start with one roll, then add another roll for each test. Remember, each penny weighs about 2.5 grams. A roll, therefore, weighs about 125 grams.

1. Place one roll in the center of your bridge. Did the bridge hold? _____

2. Did it bend the bridge? _____

3. Keep adding rolls of pennies. Remember to arrange the rolls so that the weight is spread out over the length of the bridge.

4. Record the result of each test in the table below. You can make a new table on a computer or tablet once the testing is complete. Add any notes or observations that you made while you were testing.

ARCH BRIDGE		
WEIGHT USED (PENNIES)	RESULTS	NOTES
1 roll (125 grams)		
2 rolls (250 grams)		
3 rolls (375 grams)		
4 rolls (500 grams)		
5 rolls (625 grams)		
6 rolls (750 grams)		
7 rolls (875 grams)		
8 rolls (1,000 grams)		
9 rolls (1,125 grams)		
10 rolls (1,250 grams)		

5. Try weighing some of the following materials (many are in your desk or the classroom): paperback books, small library books, stapler, box of crayons and/or markers, pencils, or a notebook. Begin testing with the lightest materials first.

6. Which materials were held by the bridge? _____

7. Illustrate your bridge below. In your illustration, include one of the loads you used to test the strength of your bridge.

★ ★ ★ SAVE YOUR ARCH BRIDGE FOR THE NEXT ACTIVITY. ★ ★ ★

CONSTRUCTING AN ARCH BRIDGE

JOURNAL ENTRY

1. What part of your arch bridge was the weakest and was the first to collapse?

   _____

   _____

   _____

2. Did your arch bridge hold more weight than the beam bridge? Describe your results.

   _____

   _____

   _____

3. What problems did you encounter in building the arch bridge?

   _____

   _____

   _____

4. What did you learn about building bridges in this activity?

   _____

   _____

   _____

5. Why did the most successful bridge in the classroom succeed? What did that bridge have that made it successful?

   _____

   _____

   _____

6. If you were doing this activity again, what would you change about your design?

   _____

   _____

   _____

DESIGN PROCESS REVIEW—CONSTRUCTING AN ARCH BRIDGE

Share your Journal Entry responses, experiences, and suggestions with the class during the discussion led by your teacher.

CONSTRUCTING A TRUSS BRIDGE

(This activity builds on the previous lesson and incorporates the design features of a truss bridge. You will want to use and repair your arch bridge before adding the truss.)

A truss bridge uses side supports in a triangular arrangement to increase the efficiency, durability, and weight-holding capacity of a bridge. The trusses can take on several different forms. However, the triangle is usually considered the strongest, most efficient geometric figure for supporting weight. These triangles will be equilateral triangles or right triangles.

TEAM MATERIALS
- 12 penny rolls
- arch bridges (from previous activity)
- masking tape
- scissors
- sewing pins
- straws

Directions:

1. Repair your arch bridge as best you can. Make sure your pins are holding the straws firmly in place. Reapply or replace the small pieces of tape you used to connect the bridge sections. Repair or replace broken or badly damaged straws.

2. Start at one end and one side of the bridge. Use pins or tape to connect one straw to the deck of the beam bridge so that it sticks straight up. Pin a second straw to the deck, 7 inches (18 cm) from the first straw (at the end of the first section of your beam bridge). Move the top of these two straws toward each other until they form a triangle sticking into the air.

3. Pin the ends of the two straws together to form the triangle.

4. Pin or tape a straw straight up into the air, next to the one at the base of the triangle. Add a second straw at the end of the second section like you did in the first section. Pin these 2 straws together to form a second triangle.

5. Repeat the above steps to form a third triangle in the third section.

N A M E _____

CONSTRUCTING A TRUSS BRIDGE

Directions *(cont.)*

6. Use one straw to connect the tips of the first two triangles. (You can use the pins already there to attach this straw.)

7. Connect the second and third triangles in the same manner.

8. Repeat what you did on this side of the bridge by adding and connecting straws on the other side, in the same way.

9. Use one straw to connect the top points (vertices) of the first two triangles at the front of the bridge. The triangles now form a triangular prism.

10. Use a straw to connect the two middle triangles and another to connect the two last triangles. Your final truss bridge should look like the illustration below.

11. If needed, cover the flat deck of the bridge as you did in the first activity with three large index cards, pieces of poster board, or pieces of Bristol board cut to fit each section.

12. Cut a piece of masking tape 3 mm by 3 cm long to attach the front of the first card to a straw and one more to attach the back of the card. Do the same for the second card in the middle section and the third card at the rear of the bridge.

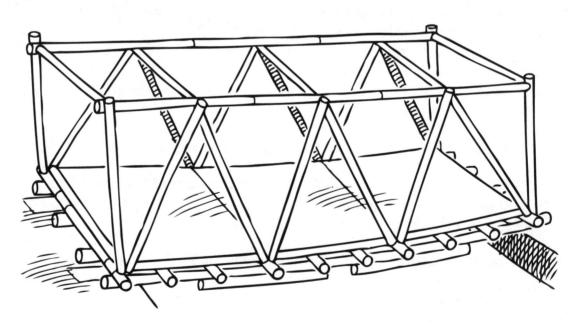

CONSTRUCTING A TRUSS BRIDGE

TESTING THE TRUSS BRIDGE

The bridges could be tested individually as the class observes. You have 12 rolls of pennies to use as testing weights. Start with one roll, then add another roll for each test. Each penny weighs about 2.5 grams. A roll, therefore, weighs about 125 grams.

COMPARISON TESTING RESULTS

1. Place one roll in the center of your bridge. Did the bridge hold? _____
2. Did it bend the bridge? _____
3. Keep adding rolls of pennies. Arrange the rolls so that the weight is spread out over the length of the bridge.
4. Record the result of each test in the table below. You can make a new table on a computer or tablet once the testing is complete. Add any notes or observations that you made while testing.

TRUSS BRIDGE		
WEIGHT USED (PENNIES)	RESULTS	NOTES
1 roll (125 grams)		
2 rolls (250 grams)		
3 rolls (375 grams)		
4 rolls (500 grams)		
5 rolls (625 grams)		
6 rolls (750 grams)		
7 rolls (875 grams)		
8 rolls (1,000 grams)		
9 rolls (1,125 grams)		
10 rolls (1,250 grams)		
11 rolls (1,375 grams)		
12 rolls (1,500 grams)		

5. Did the bridge collapse, or did it hold all 12 penny rolls when they were carefully arranged on the bridge? _____
6. What section of your bridge was the weakest and therefore the first to collapse? _____
7. Illustrate your bridge below. In your illustration, include one of the loads you used that tested the strength of your bridge.

★ ★ ★ SAVE YOUR TRUSS BRIDGE FOR THE NEXT ACTIVITY. ★ ★ ★

Ⓝ Ⓐ Ⓜ Ⓔ _____

CONSTRUCTING A TRUSS BRIDGE

JOURNAL ENTRY

1. How well did your truss bridge work in comparison to the beam and arch bridges?

   _____

   _____

   _____

2. Did you think your truss bridge was sturdier and stronger than the beam or arch bridge? Explain your reasons.

   _____

   _____

   _____

3. Where have you seen a truss bridge? Have you seen one in your neighborhood, on vacation, or on television?

   _____

   _____

   _____

4. Have you ever ridden over or walked on a truss bridge? When and where?

   _____

   _____

   _____

5. What types of bridges have you seen in your neighborhood or community?

   _____

   _____

   _____

6. What bridges have you seen personally or on TV? What kind of bridges are they?

   _____

   _____

   _____

DESIGN PROCESS REVIEW—CONSTRUCTING A TRUSS BRIDGE

Share your Journal Entry responses and your other experiences and observations with your classmates in a discussion led by your teacher.

NAME _____

BUILD A BETTER BRIDGE

You will work in teams to create your own bridge based on what you've learned in the previous activities. You may choose to build longer, stronger, bigger or smaller versions of the three types you worked with in previous units. You might choose to create a bowed arch version of the arch bridge or to try a suspension bridge. You might also try a design of your own creation. Use the Design Process Worksheet on page 5 to help guide you through the process of designing and building your bridge.

The suggested activity below is designed to help you get started if you don't have a specific idea in mind.

SUGGESTED MATERIALS
- 12 rolls of pennies
- fishing line (10 pound test or stronger)
- index cards, poster board, or Bristol board
- masking tape
- modeling clay
- rulers
- scissors
- sewing pins
- thin straws
- wooden barbeque skewers

CHALLENGE ACTIVITY—BUILD A SUSPENSION BRIDGE

Three factors affect a suspension bridge. The factors are the **_dead load_**, the **_live load_**, and the **_environment_**.

1. **The dead load is the weight of the bridge itself.**
2. **The live load are the people and materials being moved across the bridge.**
3. **The environment is the effect of wind, rain, and weather on the bridge.**

GETTING STARTED

1. Build a beam bridge as you did in the first activity or repair the one you have.

2. Gather two wood skewers. Attach each wood skewer to either side of one end of the bridge, with the points extending down about 2 inches (5 cm) below the deck of the bridge. Use two pieces of masking tape—3 mm wide by 4 cm long—to attach the wood skewers upright to the straws at the base of the bridge.

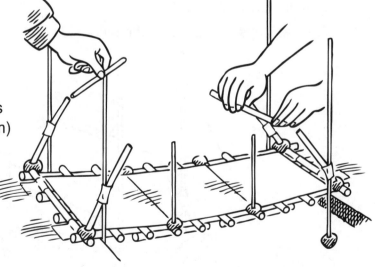

BUILD A BETTER BRIDGE

CHALLENGE ACTIVITY—BUILD A SUSPENSION BRIDGE *(cont.)*

GETTING STARTED *(cont.)*

3. Attach two more wood skewers to the other side of the bridge in the same manner.

4. Use about 1 to 2 ounces of modeling clay to form a solid ball. Insert one skewer point into the clay ball.

5. Make three more similar clay balls and insert the remaining 3 pillars into the 3 remaining clay balls. (**A**)

6. Make four more clay balls. Place each clay ball about 10 cm from each of the four wooden poles of the bridge. (**B**)

7. Place a shorter skewer in each of the clay balls, facing away from the bridges. They will be braces to make the bridge stronger.

8. Take a piece of fishing line about 18 inches (45 cm) long and tie one end to one of the short wood skewers, in the middle of the bridge. Tie the knot securely. Pull it firmly to the top of the tall skewer (**1**) attached to the same end and side of the bridge. Then tie the line firmly about 1 inch (2.5 cm) from the top of the tall skewer.

9. Tie the fishing line from the top of the tall skewer number 1 and tape it to the desk about 5 inches from the base of the bridge.

10. Repeat steps 8 and 9 using tall skewer number **2**.

11. Take a fishing line about 25 inches long and attach it to the small skewer in step 8. Then attach it with a tight knot to the top of the second skewer on the same side of the bridge. Pull the line tightly and tie the knot about 3 cm from the top of tall skewer number **3**.

12. Take the fishing line from the top of skewer number 3 and tape it to the desk about 5 inches from the base of the bridge.

13. Repeat steps 11 and 12 on the other side of the bridge.

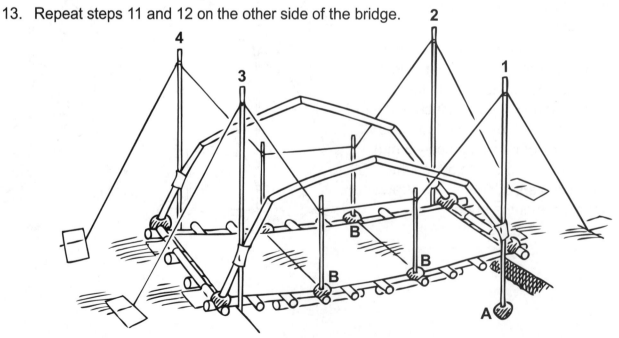

Ⓝ Ⓐ Ⓜ Ⓔ _____

BUILD A BETTER BRIDGE

CHALLENGE ACTIVITY—TESTING THE SUSPENSION BRIDGE

Use the same penny rolls as you did in the previous activities. Record the results below.

1. Place one roll in the center on your bridge. Did the bridge hold? _____
2. Did it bend the bridge? _____
3. Keep adding rolls of pennies. Arrange the rolls so that the weight is spread out over the length of the bridge.
4. Record the result of each test in the table below. You can make a new table on a computer or tablet once the testing is complete. Add any notes or observations that you made while testing.

SUSPENSION BRIDGE		
WEIGHT USED (PENNIES)	RESULTS	NOTES
1 roll (125 grams)		
2 rolls (250 grams)		
3 rolls (375 grams)		
4 rolls (500 grams)		
5 rolls (625 grams)		
6 rolls (750 grams)		
7 rolls (875 grams)		
8 rolls (1,000 grams)		
9 rolls (1,125 grams)		
10 rolls (1,250 grams)		
11 rolls (1,375 grams)		
12 rolls (1,500 grams)		

5. Did the bridge collapse or did it hold all 12 rolls of pennies when they were carefully arranged on the bridge?

_____

6. Describe what happened to the fishing line "suspension cables" as the weight was added.

_____

7. Illustrate your bridge in the box below. Include the rolls of pennies in the positions they were distributed across the bridge.

 _____

BUILD A BETTER BRIDGE

CHALLENGE ACTIVITY—JOURNAL ENTRY

Use a computer, tablet, or other device to write paragraphs for each topic. Use complete sentences and describe your experiences clearly.

PARAGRAPH 1

Describe your bridge. Were you successful in completing the project? Did the bridge carry a heavy load? How did you test it?

PARAGRAPH 2

What did you learn in this bridge-building unit over the last four activities? Give detailed information.

PARAGRAPH 3

Would you like to be a bridge engineer after your experiences in this unit? Why or why not? Explain your reasons.

PARAGRAPH 4

Which team do you think had the best or most successful bridge? Why did you select this bridge? Provide several reasons.

PARAGRAPH 5

Respond to these questions by referring back to the activities you completed in this unit.

1. *What are the main types of bridge designs?*

2. *Which style of bridge is strongest?*

3. *How does a truss bridge distribute weight?*

4. *Why can an arch bridge carry more weight than a beam bridge?*

5. *How does a suspension bridge work?*

DESIGN PROCESS REVIEW—BUILD A BETTER BRIDGE

Share your experiences, insights, ideas, and reflections about bridge building in the class discussion your teacher leads to culminate this unit.

Common Core State Standards

Each lesson meets one or more of the following Common Core State Standards © Copyright 2010. National Governors Association Center for Best Practices and Council of Chief State School Officers. All rights reserved. For more information about the Common Core State Standards, go to *http://www.corestandards.org/* or *http://www.teachercreated.com/standards*.

Reading Informational Text Standards	Pages
Key Ideas and Details	
ELA.RI.5.3 Explain the relationships or interactions between two or more individuals, events, ideas, or concepts in a historical, scientific, or technical text based on specific information in the text.	22–35, 39–51, 55–75, 79–95, 99–119, 123–139, 143–158
Craft and Structure	
ELA.RI.5.4 Determine the meaning of general academic and domain-specific words and phrases in a text relevant to a grade 5 topic or subject area.	15, 19, 21, 37, 38, 53, 54, 77, 78, 97, 98, 121, 122, 141, 142
Integration of Knowledge and Ideas	
ELA.RI.5.7 Draw on information from multiple print or digital sources, demonstrating the ability to locate an answer to a question quickly or to solve a problem efficiently.	21, 38, 54, 78, 98, 122, 142
ELA.RI.5.9 Integrate information from several texts on the same topic in order to write or speak about the subject knowledgeably.	22–35, 39–51, 55–75, 79–95, 99–119, 123–139, 143–158
Range of Reading and Level of Text Complexity	
ELA.RI.5.10 By the end of the year, read and comprehend informational texts, including history/social studies, science, and technical texts, at the high end of the grades 4–5 text complexity band independently and proficiently.	22–35, 39–51, 55–75, 79–95, 99–119, 123–139, 143–158

Writing Standards	Pages
Text Types and Purposes	
ELA.W.5.2 Write informative/explanatory texts to examine a topic and convey ideas and information clearly.	25, 29, 32, 35, 41, 44, 47, 51, 60, 64, 69, 75, 83, 87, 91, 95, 102, 107, 112, 117–118, 119, 127, 133, 136, 139, 147, 150, 154, 158
Production and Distribution of Writing	
ELA.W.5.4 Produce clear and coherent writing in which the development and organization are appropriate to task, purpose, and audience.	25, 29, 32, 35, 41, 44, 47, 51, 60, 64, 69, 75, 83, 87, 91, 95, 102, 107, 112, 117–118, 119, 127, 133, 136, 139, 147, 150, 154, 158
ELA.W.5.6 With some guidance and support from adults, use technology, including the Internet, to produce and publish writing as well as to interact and collaborate with others; demonstrate sufficient command of keyboarding skills to type a minimum of two pages in a single sitting.	21, 35, 38, 45, 51, 54, 75, 78, 88, 95, 98, 106, 119, 122, 139, 142, 145, 149, 153, 157, 158
Research to Build and Present Knowledge	
ELA.W.5.7 Conduct short research projects that use several sources to build knowledge through investigation of different aspects of a topic.	21–25, 26–29, 30–32, 33–35, 39–41, 42–44, 45–47, 48–51, 55–60, 61–64, 65–69, 70–75, 79–83, 84–87, 88–91, 92–95, 99–102, 103–107, 108–112, 113–119, 123–127, 128–133, 134–136, 137–139, 143–147, 148–150, 151–154, 155–158
ELA.W.5.9 Draw evidence from literary or informational texts to support analysis, reflection, and research.	20, 21, 22–35, 38, 39–51, 54, 55–75, 78, 79–95, 98, 99–119, 122, 123–139, 142, 143–158

Speaking & Listening Standards	Pages
Comprehension and Collaboration	
ELA.SL.5.1 Engage effectively in a range of collaborative discussions (one-on-one, in groups, and teacher-led) with diverse partners on *grade 5 topics and texts*, building on others' ideas and expressing their own clearly.	25, 29, 32, 35, 41, 44, 47, 51, 60, 64, 69, 75, 83, 87, 91, 95, 102, 107, 112, 117–118, 119, 127, 133, 136, 139, 147, 150, 154, 158
Presentation of Knowledge and Ideas	
ELA.SL.5.4 Report on a topic or text or present an opinion, sequencing ideas logically and using appropriate facts and relevant, descriptive details to support main ideas or themes; speak clearly at an understandable pace.	25, 29, 32, 35, 41, 44, 47, 51, 60, 64, 69, 75, 83, 87, 91, 95, 102, 107, 112, 117–118, 119, 127, 133, 136, 139, 147, 150, 154, 158

Next Generation Science Standards

5. Structure and Properties of Matter	Pages
Students who demonstrate understanding can:	
5-PS1-1. Develop a model to describe that matter is made of particles too small to be seen.	
Unit 2—Air and Water (Challenge Activity—Invention) Air, Water, Wind, and Heat	48–51
5-PS1-2. Measure and graph quantities to provide evidence that regardless of the type of change that occurs when heating, cooling, or mixing substances, the total weight of matter is conserved.	
Unit 2—Air and Water (Make Your Own Cloud)	39–41
Unit 2—Air and Water (Bottle Thermometer)	42–44
5-PS1-3. Make observations and measurements to identify materials based on their properties.	
Unit 2—Air and Water (Make Your Own Cloud)	39–41
Unit 2—Air and Water (Bottle Thermometer)	42–44

5. Space Systems: Stars and the Solar System	Pages
Students who demonstrate understanding can:	
5-PS2-1. Support an argument that the gravitational force exerted by Earth on objects is directed down.	
Unit 6—Working with Motors (Motorized Marbles)	134–136

3-5. Engineering Design	Pages
Students who demonstrate understanding can:	
3-5-ETS1-1. Define a simple design problem reflecting a need or a want that includes specified criteria for success and constraints on materials, time, or cost.	
Unit 1—Electric Circuits	22–35
Unit 2—Air and Water	39–51
Unit 3—Reflection and Refraction	55–75
Unit 4—Water Pressure and Capillarity	79–95
Unit 5—Magnetism and Electromagnetism	99–119
Unit 6—Working with Motors	123–139
Unit 7—Building Bridges	143–158
3-5-ETS1-2. Generate and compare multiple possible solutions to a problem based on how well each is likely to meet the criteria and constraints of the problem.	
Unit 1—Electric Circuits	22–35
Unit 2—Air and Water	39–51
Unit 3—Reflection and Refraction	55–75
Unit 4—Water Pressure and Capillarity	79–95
Unit 5—Magnetism and Electromagnetism	99–119
Unit 6—Working with Motors	123–139
Unit 7—Building Bridges	143–158
3-5-ETS1-3. Plan and carry out fair tests in which variables are controlled and failure points are considered to identify aspects of a model or prototype that can be improved.	
Unit 1—Electric Circuits	22–35
Unit 2—Air and Water	39–51
Unit 3—Reflection and Refraction	55–75
Unit 4—Water Pressure and Capillarity	79–95
Unit 5—Magnetism and Electromagnetism	99–119
Unit 6—Working with Motors	123–139
Unit 7—Building Bridges	143–158